POLITICAL FREEDOM

BY THE SAME AUTHOR

The Liberal College
Freedom and the College
Philosophy
The Experimental College
What Does America Mean?
Education Between Two Worlds

POLITICAL FREEDOM

THE CONSTITUTIONAL POWERS OF THE PEOPLE

by Alexander Meiklejohn

With a Foreword by Malcolm Pitman Sharp,
School of Law, University of Chicago

GREENWOOD PRESS, PUBLISHERS
WESTPORT, CONNECTICUT

Library of Congress Cataloging in Publication Data

Meiklejohn, Alexander, 1872-1964.
    Political freedom.

    "Part one contains, with a minor change, the text of
the book Free speech and its relation to self-government,
published in 1948."
    Reprint of the 1st ed. published by Harper, New York.
    Bibliography: p.
    1. Liberty of speech--United States.   I.   Title.
[JC591.M42   1979]   323.44'3'0973   78-27616
ISBN 0-313-20907-3

This edition published in 1960 by Harper & Brothers, Publishers,
New York

Reprinted with the permission of Harper & Row, Publishers, Inc.

Reprinted in 1979 by Greenwood Press, Inc.
51 Riverside Avenue, Westport, CT 06880

Printed in the United States of America

10 9 8 7 6 5 4 3 2 1

To Walton Hale Hamilton

whose pupil I became many years ago when
we were together at Amherst College

INTRODUCTORY NOTE

This book consists of two parts. Part One contains, with a minor change, the text of the book *Free Speech and Its Relation to Self-Government,* published in 1948. Part Two is a collection of papers, written between 1948 and 1958, in which the argument of the original book is developed and, in some measure, transformed.

A new Foreword by Malcolm Sharp relates both Parts to recent developments in Supreme Court doctrine.

ACKNOWLEDGMENTS

We are grateful to the following periodicals for permission to reprint articles originally published in their pages:

Bulletin of the American Association of University Professors, for "The Teaching of Intellectual Freedom" (xxxviii, 1, Spring 1952).

The Bulletin of the Atomic Scientists, for "Integrity of the Universities—How to Defend It" (June 1953).

The Harvard Crimson, for a letter in reply to Professors Sutherland and Chafee (January 1954).

The Nation, for "The Limits of Congressional Authority" (December 13, 1953).

The New York Times Magazine, for "Should Communists Be Allowed to Teach?" (March 27, 1949). (Reprinted herein under the title "Professors on Probation.")

CONTENTS

FOREWORD

BY MALCOLM SHARP
School of Law, University of Chicago

WHEN I first read these lectures ten years ago, and discussed them with their author, I was fully persuaded of the soundness of the position taken. Moreover, the discussion indicated how practical and manageable, in their application to specific cases, are the distinctions which the author has stated generally. As a reader and a hearer, I was delighted, as I had been more than thirty years before when I was a student in Mr. Meiklejohn's classes at Amherst. Now that I am honored by being asked to write a preface, I find that besides pleasure, another feeling appears—one which I first met in 1916 and have experienced since. Mr. Meiklejohn is not one to leave his students in peace. His classes were like nothing I have ever experienced, not only for pleasure, but for stimulus and disturbance. Now that I am not simply reading and listening, but responding, I feel again that tension and interest which are the work of an incomparable teacher.

I am back in his classroom. It is true that I have become a lawyer, and acquired a little of what some members of my profession might consider their peculiar qualifications for considering a book on law. I think that they would be mistaken. On the great questions of law, the lawyer must still go to school to the philosopher.

Since I have returned to his classroom, I have somehow again become aware of the tension in Mr. Meiklejohn's thought, the paradox that is there implicit in the seemingly direct statement,

xi

the contradiction and multiplicity as well as the consistency and the simplicity of things.

If the reader becomes a fellow student, he will stop and wonder, and appreciate as well, while he reads. He may be interested, moreover, in recalling the vindication which the thesis of these lectures has received in the years since they were first given.

1

First at Amherst and later at Wisconsin, I found Mr. Meiklejohn going back most often to Plato and to Kant. What these two philosophers appear to have said about the non-human part of the universe is not here Mr. Meiklejohn's concern; indeed, his one observation here about the non-human part of the universe reminds us that he is not to be too easily classified. His view about the nature and functions of the truth, and his conception of man as markedly distinguished by his intelligence from all the other animals, have, however, a classical history. His argument about the meaning of the First Amendment of the Constitution is not based immediately—at least so he says—on a theory about the nature of man. Yet the reader will find that the theory of human nature appearing throughout the lectures makes an important contribution to the author's theory of the meaning of the text of the Amendment, and its relation to a scheme of rational self-government.

The student, as in his college days and often since, has put some questions to the teacher; and the teacher has allowed the student to quote his answers.

THE TEACHER: It is not easy for the non-lawyer who writes this book to think of Professor Sharp as his student in matters of law. But being cast in the role of teacher, I must try to play it. And in doing so, I recall that, when theories are debated, the teacher's duty is not to give authoritative answers, but rather to clarify questions by challenging their assumptions. He should seek not to end a discussion, but to start it, or to keep it going. The following replies have that intention.

QUESTION 1: The argument here does not concern itself with the adjustment of conflicting interests or the comparison of consequences. The interpretation of the Constitution here advocated will presumably have some undesirable results along with the desirable ones. Must not the interests affected and the expected results be listed and compared?

ANSWER: The listing and comparing of the merits and defects of the Constitution, though exceedingly important on other occasions, is, I think, foreign to my present argument. We are not adopting or amending our Plan of Government. We are asking what, in its deepest meaning, the present plan is.

The reader who is acquainted with the hard-fought conflict between the Pragmatist and Idealist philosophies of the last fifty or sixty years will recognize how tightly packed are the controversial and confusing issues enclosed within this question. I shall try to deal with those issues as one who thinks himself to be both Pragmatist and Idealist.

I am sure that any interpretations of the First Amendment, including that of these lectures, will have, if adopted, undesirable as well as desirable results. When we govern we choose. We seek to win one value by sacrificing another. And, it must be added, we make mistakes.

But further, in a society like our own, where forms of belief and communication are changing ever more rapidly and radically, the justifiability of the First Amendment or of our interpretation of it must always be kept open to constant and critical reconsideration. We may never cease to ask the question, "Is it just and wise?"

These two sets of considerations make it clear that with respect to any provision of the Constitution, "the interests affected and the expected results" *must* be "listed and compared," re-listed and re-compared.

It is at this point that my questioner remarks that in the book which he presents to the reader, no such listing and comparing have been done. To this observation two replies are, I think, valid and necessary.

First, the questioner knows that on many other occasions, I have expressed the conviction that, as measured by its consequences, our national program of religious and political freedom has been one of the greatest and most useful of human achievements.

But second, this book is written, not to praise or to justify the First Amendment, but to discover what it means. Finding out what a principle intends to say seems to me prior, though not alternative, to judging its usefulness and truth.

QUESTION 2: You seem to say that the hypothesis that *intelligence can control* is the critical hypothesis of self-government. As you know, the influence of other factors in government was recognized by the framers of our Constitution and their contemporaries. The hidden work of irrational impulses has been studied in recent years, and its influence seen in the conduct of affairs. It is possible to infer your view of these matters, from the course of the argument; but it would be interesting to have an explicit observation about them.

ANSWER: Our American venture in self-government is not based on "assurance" that we are intelligent enough to be free, but only on the "hope" that our minds can carry the responsibilities which the Constitution assigns to them. As my questioner says, it is well known that among the writers of the Constitution there were grievous fears at this point. And further, our current studies of the irrational elements in our decision-making are increasing those fears. Unless our national education can be raised to much higher levels, it is possible that our enormous wealth and power will be used to weaken intelligence rather than to strengthen it. Our self-governing is not, then, based on assurance of success. It is, as Mr. Justice

Holmes has told us, an "experiment." We have only a chance, but one which is worth fighting for—*with our minds.*

QUESTION 3: You make a persuasive distinction between the freedom to speak on public matters protected without qualification by the First Amendment and the "liberty" to speak on private matters protected by the Due Process Clauses, subject to control by "due process of law." In your discussion of radio you emphasize the distinction by saying that here private speaking not only may but should be subject to control. The question of policy is not the same as the question of constitutional validity. Some would say, however, that freedom of speech is most likely to be given full protection against group pressures and government alike, in a society in which other freedoms, the "liberties," are given all the protection consistent with elementary order. I judge you have some doubt, at least, about that view. How much, if any, force does it have? Are the two sets of immunities, the freedoms and the liberties, quite distinct ?

ANSWER: Yes, I believe that, constitutionally, the public "powers" by which citizens govern themselves are "quite distinct" from the private "liberties" which, by corporate action, those citizens grant to themselves and others, as individuals whom they govern. The "freedom" of the First Amendment and the "liberty" of the Fifth are, I think, "quite distinct" in kind and in constitutional status.

Since you ask for my opinion on the question whether or not a policy of relatively unregulated private enterprise is more favorable to political freedom than is a policy of active governmental regulation, I will try to indicate my point of view. On the whole, the "liberties" of what we call "Free Enterprise" are, I think, destructive of the "freedoms" of a self-governing society. The unregulated self-seeking of the profit-makers is much more dangerous in its effect upon the morality and intelligence of the citizen than that *participation in regulatory action* for the common good to which free enterprise has so often shown itself hostile. In the first edition of this book I cited, as a striking example of the disastrous effect of giving great "liberty" to private enterprise, the handing over of the use of the air waves to radio corporations. But privately sponsored television has proved to be even more deadly. Those business controls of communication are, day by day, year by year, destroying and degrading our intelligence and our taste by the use of instruments which should be employed in educating and uplifting them.

QUESTION 4: You say that teachers and others in Germany under occupation after the Second World War had no moral claim to the kind of freedom of speech protected by our Constitution, since they were not part of a self-governing community. Does this observation indicate a significant general principle? What other cases of the sort might be considered or imagined?

ANSWER: Yes, there is here a significant principle which must be recognized: Political freedom, as we have it, exists, and exists only, in virtue of a compact by which it is agreed that all the members of our national group shall share, with equal status, in responsibility for the making of decisions concerning the common good. Freedom of this kind does not come to us as a gift or an endowment. It comes only as we create institutions of self-government and maintain them by exercising the powers which are granted to us, by assuming the obligations which are laid upon us. The text of the first edition mentions a few types of social grouping which are not self-governing in the political sense. There are many others. For purposes of illustration we could take a family, a university football team, a business corporation of the usual type. The owners, managers, and workers who make up the membership of a business group are *not* equal in status with respect to the governing of their enterprise. The group is not self-governing as free citizens are under the Constitution.

One final difficulty may appear to a student. Anyone who has studied contracts will be fascinated by Mr. Meiklejohn's theory of a social contract entered into by successive generations and changing in its meanings with the changing contexts of different times. On the other hand, anyone who has also studied constitutional law and constitutional history will realize the more clearly that lawyers have a singular knack of making changes which suit their notions of policy in ways which render the process of change invisible to the ordinary eye. If, for example, judges are to continue to have the last word about the Constitution, are we to trust them to mold it in accordance with their views of the needs of the time? Experience indicates that with the lawyer's skill they will mold it imperceptibly in their own images. Other government agencies, advised by lawyers, may do the same thing with legislation and sometimes with the Constitution. A lawyer may think that his fellow lawyers in power need to be controlled by a text with a fixed meaning.

Here, at any rate, this particular student is satisfied that the objection does not affect Mr. Meiklejohn's thesis about the First Amendment. Little is known about the context in which the First Amendment was first written and read. The word "abridge" has one familiar meaning of "decrease." If Congress must not "decrease" freedom of speech, the reference may be to existing law, and the most likely law for reference would be the eighteenth century common law of the Colonies and of England. That common law, after something of a battle, excluded prior restraints on the publication of ideas, but in its application to American conditions, it was otherwise at best indeterminate.

The difficulty has not yet been fully investigated, but an alert younger student, very much under Mr. Meiklejohn's influence, is trying to explore the matter without bias. Mr. George Anastaplo has found, for example in Blackstone, instances in which "abridge" is clearly taken to mean "restrict," and to refer to a natural or ideal state of law. This way of speaking would be a reasonable one for eighteenth century lawyers. While it is not Mr. Meiklejohn's way of speaking, it has some similarity to the course of his thought. And it makes it possible for a lawyer skeptical about his own profession's self-restraint to recognize that at the very least the ambiguity of the word "abridging" in the First Amendment is such as to make appropriate Mr. Meiklejohn's lawyerlike and—still better—philosophical treatment of the meaning of this critical constitutional provision.

The student may say that if he has to choose he would feel that the historical meaning of the Constitution should control, but he is well satisfied with a result in which that coincides with Mr. Meiklejohn's philosophical meaning. The teacher would reply that this is indeed fortunate, but if there were a difference, the philosophical and—he might add—the contemporary meanings are the ones which a reasonable philosopher must prefer.

2

Whatever its philosophical characteristics, the thesis of these lectures has been supported by our experience in the years since they were first delivered.

In 1948, the year of their publication, the time of pervasive loyalty proceedings before committees and boards was not far advanced. The requirement of non-Communist affidavits for union leaders as a condition of access to the National Labor Relations Board was soon to be followed by the conviction of Communist Party leaders for conspiracy to teach and advocate the violent overthrow of our government. This was followed, in turn, and for some in a way confirmed, by the spy cases. In 1954, as we can now see, the emotional factors in the sequence of events began to lose some of their effect. If Mr. Meiklejohn's views had been accepted in 1948 by the community, its Congress, or the Courts, individuals would have been spared injustice. The coun-

try would have avoided a period of exaggerated fear and hostility, adding its stimulus to the cold war and the war, and
threatening sane standards of administration.

Since 1954 there has been a change in our emotional tone and
a new judicial approach to legal problems. We may hope that
both will be permanent. So far as views like those expressed by
Mr. Meiklejohn appear in the Supreme Court, we see the value
of the position taken in the lectures. When we recognize the
possibility that a time like the six years before 1954 may again
occur, we see again, in a different way, the value of the freedom
of speech and sanity of mind advocated in this book.

It is to be hoped that the author's views will receive further
consideration by the Court for whose position he shows such
profound respect. Recent opinions prepare the way for his increasing influence, or at least for the increasing influence of
opinions close to his.

In two of the 1957 cases which seem to indicate a new judicial
approach to problems of freedom of speech, ideas approaching
Mr. Meiklejohn's were expressed. One involved a union organ-
izer and Congress and the other a scholar and a state legislature.
It was held that a witness before a committee or similar agency
must be given, by some means, a fair basis for judging whether
refusal to answer questions would be illegal. The requirement is
comparable to the constitutional requirement of reasonable clarity in the definitions of crimes.

In both the 1957 cases ideas had been inquired into by procedure now held unconstitutional. Chief Justice Warren wrote
the opinions of the Court in both cases, and Mr. Justice Frankfurter concurred in special opinions.

The Chief Justice said, "The mere summoning of a witness
and compelling him to testify, against his will, about his beliefs,
expressions or associations is a measure of governmental interference. And when those forced revelations concern matters that
are unorthodox, unpopular, or even hateful to the general public,
the reaction in the life of the witness may be disastrous. . . .

Those who are identified by witnesses and thereby placed in the same glare of publicity are equally subject to public stigma, scorn and obloquy. Beyond that, there is the more subtle and immeasurable effect upon those who tend to adhere to the most orthodox and uncontroversial views and associations in order to avoid a similar fate at some future time."

Mr. Justice Frankfurter said, "These pages need not be burdened with proof, based on the testimony of a cloud of impressive witnesses, of the dependence of a free society on free universities. This means the exclusion of governmental intervention in the intellectual life of a university."

On the same day the Court held that the activities of a Communist group teaching and advocating revolution as something to be believed in, but not to be undertaken, were not a criminal conspiracy. Its earlier opinion in the first Communist leaders' conspiracy case was strictly limited.

Mr. Justice Black, while urging that the Court should go further than it did in finally disposing of the cases of some of the defendants, concurred in other respects with the opinion of the Court. In an opinion in which Mr. Justice Douglas concurred, Mr. Justice Black made explicit his approach, which had appeared in earlier opinions, to a position very much like Mr. Meiklejohn's. Citing these lectures he said: "I believe that the First Amendment forbids Congress to punish people for talking about public affairs, whether or not such discussion incites to action, legal or illegal."

Indeed, in view of the ambiguity of the word "incites" in its application to various circumstances, it may be that Mr. Justice Black is going further in protecting freedom of speech than Mr. Meiklejohn, in conversation, has indicated he would be ready to go. Abstract advocacy is not always easy to tell from "incitement," nor can incitement always be easily distinguished from "command." When we pass to the communication referred to by the term "command," we come to the type of communication which any state worthy of its name will of course suppress, as it will suppress racial violence or rioting. It is the discussion of political ideas, often involving warmth and enthusiasm, which is always to be protected against our officials, in the view of Mr. Meiklejohn and Mr. Justice Black alike.

Last year, state legislation conditioning churches' and veterans' tax exemption on oaths and, if necessary, proof of freedom from subversive ideas was held invalid. Again Mr. Justice Black, with whom Mr. Justice Douglas concurred, wrote an eloquent concurring opinion recalling earlier opinions in which he had expressed similar views. In addition, referring to the First Amendment, the Justice gave a concise key to an argument which is perhaps not exactly the same as the one on which Mr. Meiklejohn depends, but which includes some of the same features.

"We should never forget that the freedoms secured by that Amendment—Speech, Press, Religion Petition and Assembly—are absolutely indispensable for the preservation of a free society in which government is based upon the consent of an informed citizenry and is dedicated to the protection of the rights of all, even the most despised minorities."

Mr. Meiklejohn's insight has been doubly vindicated. First, the safeguards which he proposed, in the form of an interpretation of the First Amendment, might well have saved us from some of the intolerance of recent years. And second, in the cases culminating in 1957, the Supreme Court has shown a solicitude for freedom of opinion and communication which is heartening for many citizens.

Two of this year's Supreme Court decisions have occasioned some doubt about the implications of the 1957 cases dealing with Legislative and Congressional committees and investigations. At the least the opinions in these two recent cases indicate that witnesses are thought to need only a rather limited definition of a committee's functions to help them in judging whether their rights are being invaded.

The opinions in some passages seem to go further. In a strange misapplication of the already somewhat simple versions of "in-

terest theory" current in some circles, the Court speaks of
"balancing" the "private" interests protected by the First Amendment against the "public" interest in national self-preservation.
It returns in other passages to earlier uncritical statements about
the threat of the domestic Communists, which have been cor-
rected by the course of conspiracy cases since the Court announced its wise and conservative views of conspiracy in 1957.
Further, the Court does not observe in these recent cases that
the broad though not unlimited powers of Congress and legislatures to direct investigations of matters of legislative concern
do not inevitably carry with them the power to employ methods
not necessary, often not even helpful, for their exercise. The in-
vestigative power of Congress was first clearly held to carry with
it the subpoena power in the investigation of the Teapot Dome
scandals, where a subpoena power was perhaps helpful or even
necessary. It is doubtful however whether any of the legislation
produced by the benevolent committees of the thirties or by the
committees investigating the Communists in the forties and fifties,
and the Teamsters in the fifties, owed or can ever owe anything to information resulting from the use of subpoenas in those
investigations. One may at least await with interest the appearance in practice of what seems in principle a limiting case: the
case of the witness whose record gives no preliminary indication
that he can contribute information useful to a committee, and
whose position on some such public issue as desegregation or
public housing gives rise to an inference that he is being exposed
on that account.

Subpoena powers are not necessary to enable Congressional
committees to obtain the information needed for ordinary legislative purposes. They are no more necessary to serve the educational or political campaign purposes thought by some to be
a justification for congressional investigations. As the dissenting
Justices in the recent cases said, with some force, their one constant purpose is to provide non-judicial agencies with means of
punishment in the form of exposure by procedures which are

travesties of judicial procedure. The practice is serious enough in the case of the Teamsters, whose leaders' powers may well need some moderation. When it is applied to the minorities who provide some of the leaven of our lives but who are dangerously exposed, it becomes more serious. It is here that the procedural point becomes again inextricably combined with the substantive point, which Mr. Meiklejohn insists is the important one. If we are punishing by exposure before committees who make their own substantive and procedural law as they go along, when this punishment is directed toward the communication of unpopular beliefs it becomes a critical violation of the First Amendment. Here again Mr. Justice Black, dissenting, recalls us to the wisdom of Mr. Meiklejohn's approach to this question:

> . . . The First Amendment says in no equivocal language that Congress shall pass no law abridging freedom of speech, press, assembly or petition. The activities of this Committee, authorized by Congress, do precisely that, through exposure, obloquy and public scorn. . . .
>
> I do not agree that laws directly abridging First Amendment freedoms can be justified by a congressional or judicial balancing process. . . .
>
> But even assuming what I cannot assume, that some balancing is proper in this case, I feel that the Court after stating the test ignores it completely. At most it balances the right of the Government to preserve itself, against Barenblatt's right to refrain from revealing Communist affiliations. Such a balance, however, mistakes the factors to be weighed. In the first place, it completely leaves out the real interest in Barenblatt's silence, the interest of the people as a whole in being able to join organizations, advocate causes and make political "mistakes" without later being subjected to governmental penalties for having dared to think for themselves. It is this right, the right to err politically, which keeps us strong as a Nation. . . .
>
> Moreover, I cannot agree with the Court's notion that First Amendment freedoms must be abridged in order to "preserve" our country. That notion rests on the unarticulated premise that this Nation's security hangs upon its power to punish people because of

what they think, speak or write about, or because of those with whom they associate for political purposes. . . . The First Amendment means to me, however, that the only constitutional way our Government can preserve itself is to leave its people the fullest possible freedom to praise, criticize or discuss, as they see fit, all governmental policies and to suggest, if they desire, that even its most fundamental postulates are bad and should be changed; "Therein lies the security of the Republic, the very foundation of constitutional government." . . .

It is to be hoped that the two recent cases, which do not determine the issue raised by Mr. Meiklejohn's thesis about the First Amendment, represent only a temporary qualification of the tendency toward acceptance of his views and the similar views expressed by majority and dissenting Justices in recent cases. Our unhappy experience before 1957 and the return of reason since are now supplemented in their educational effect by some of the language in these last opinions suggesting a threat to return us to the jurisprudence of 1951. Against this threat Mr. Meiklejohn has offered us a wise and sound theory of our fundamental law.

In observing that by the tests of history, logic, experience, and human value, Mr. Meiklejohn's position seems to be good law, we should not overlook the fact that for some it may have an even greater importance. In its gay and cheerful spirit as well as in its careful and serious argument, this book will serve the health and happiness of the community. It can educate the members of the community who in the end determine for us the critical issues of government.

Mr. Meiklejohn's lectures appeal to our wisdom and our intelligence as the most valuable features of the known universe. It should be noticed that one characteristic of a healthy intelligence is its opposition to the hatred, cruelty, and destruction which are less amiable features of the universe. The reticence of the lectures should not lead the reader to overlook their affirmative relation to the Christian as well as the Greek elements in our tradition.

They are the work of an incomparable teacher. At Amherst, at Wisconsin, in California, he has been the leading proponent of the most constructive features of recent thinking about education. He has taught generations of students by thoughtful example and stimulus. As he says, his philosophy of education seems to him more important as a whole than that part of it which appears here. Nevertheless, this part is of critical importance today, for both domestic and foreign policy. It is, moreover, a perfect introduction for a reader who may be prepared to read further, or to re-read, the published work of this courageous teacher.

PART ONE

FREE SPEECH AND ITS RELATION TO

SELF-GOVERNMENT

PREFACE

THE ARGUMENT of this book was first given in three lectures at the University of Chicago, under the Charles R. Walgreen Foundation for the Study of American Institutions. It was later given, in the same form, at the Law School of Yale University, at St. John's College, and, in part, as a lecture and discussion in the Great Issues Course at Dartmouth College. It is here presented with some slight changes which are intended to serve the transition from the hearing of an argument to the reading of it.

The book discusses a principle of law. It is written, however, not by a lawyer, but by a teacher. It springs from a strong conviction that a primary task of American education is to arouse and to cultivate, in all the members of the body politic, a desire to understand what our national plan of government is. The book, therefore, is a challenge to all of us, as citizens, to study the Constitution. That constitution derives whatever validity, whatever meaning, it has, not from its acceptance by our forefathers one hundred and sixty years ago, but from its acceptance by us, now. Clearly, however, we cannot, in any valid sense, "accept" the Constitution unless we know what it says. And, for that reason, every loyal citizen of the nation must join with his fellows in the attempt to interpret, in principle and in action, that provision of the Constitution which is rightly regarded as its most vital assertion, its most significant contribution to political wisdom. What do We, the People of the United States, mean when

3

we provide for the freedom of belief and of the expression of belief?

1

The First Amendment to the Constitution, as we all know, forbids the federal Congress to make any law which shall abridge the freedom of speech. In recent years, however, the government of the United States has in many ways limited the freedom of public discussion. For example, the Federal Bureau of Investigation has built up, throughout the country, a system of espionage, of secret police, by which hundreds of thousands of our people have been listed as holding this or that set of opinions. The only conceivable justification of that listing by a government agency is to provide a basis for action by the government in dealing with those persons. And that procedure reveals an attitude toward freedom of speech which is widely held in the United States. Many of us are now convinced that, under the Constitution, the government is justified in bringing pressure to bear against the holding or expressing of beliefs which are labeled "dangerous." Congress, we think, may rightly abridge the freedom of such beliefs.

Again, the legislative committees, federal and state, which have been appointed to investigate un-American activities, express the same interpretation of the Constitution. All the inquirings and questionings of those committees are based upon the assumption that certain forms of political opinion and advocacy should be, and legitimately may be, suppressed. And, further, the Department of Justice, acting on the same assumption, has recently listed some sixty or more organizations, association with which may be taken by the government to raise the question of "disloyalty" to the United States. And finally, the President's Loyalty Order, moving with somewhat uncertain steps, follows the same road. We are officially engaged in the suppression of "dangerous" speech.

Now, these practices would seem to be flatly contradictory of the First Amendment. Are they? What do we mean when we say that "Congress shall make no law . . . abridging the freedom of speech . . . ?" What is this "freedom of speech" which we guard against invasion by our chosen and authorized representatives? Why may not a man be prevented from speaking if, in the judgment of Congress, his ideas are hostile and harmful to the general welfare of the nation? Are we, for example, required by the First Amendment to give men freedom to advocate the abolition of the First Amendment? Are we bound to grant freedom of speech to those who, if they had the power, would refuse it to us? The First Amendment, taken literally, seems to answer, "Yes" to those questions. It seems to say that no speech, however dangerous, may, for that reason, be suppressed. But the Federal Bureau of Investigation, the un-American Activities committees, the Department of Justice, the President, are, at the same time, answering "No" to the same question. Which answer is right? What is the valid American doctrine concerning the freedom of speech?

2

Throughout our history, the need of clear and reasonable answering of that question has been very urgent. In fact, under our system of dealing with problems of domestic policy by "party" discussion and "party" action, the demand for such clarity and reasonableness is basic to our "democratic" way of life. But, with the ending of World War II, that demand has taken on a new, and even greater, urgency. Our nation has now assumed, or has had thrust upon it by Fate, a new role. We have taken leadership in the advocating of freedom of expression and of communication, not only at home, but also throughout the world. In the waging of that campaign we Americans have made many accusations against our enemies in war, hot or cold. But our most furious and righteous charge has been that they have suppressed, and are suppressing, the free exchange of information and of ideas. That evil drawing of a smoke curtain, we have declared, we will not tolerate. We will not submit to it within our own borders. We will not allow it abroad if, by legitimate means, we can prevent it. We are determined that, with respect to the freedom of its communications, the human world shall be a single community.

Now, the assuming of that high and heavy responsibility for a political principle requires of us, first of all, that we understand what the principle is. We must think for it as well as fight for it. No fighting, however successful, will help to establish freedom unless the winners know what freedom is. What, then—we citizens under the Constitution must ask—what do we mean when we utter the flaming proclamation of the First Amendment? Do we mean that speaking may be suppressed or that it shall not be suppressed? And, in either case, on what grounds has the decision been made?

3

The issue here presented has been dramatically, though perhaps not very effectively, thrust upon the attention of the citizens of the United States by a recent order of the Attorney General. That order restricts the freedom of speech of temporary foreign visitors to our shores. It declares that certain classes of visitors are forbidden, except by special permission, to engage in public discussion of public policy while they are among us. Why may we not hear what these men from other countries, other systems of government, have to say? For what purpose does the Attorney General impose limits upon their speaking, upon our hearing? The plain truth is that he is seeking to protect the minds of the citizens of this free nation of ours from the influence of assertions, of doubts, of questions, of plans, of principles which the government judges to be too "dangerous" for us to hear. He is afraid that we, whose agent he is, will be led astray by opinions which are alien and subversive. Do We, the

People of the United States, wish to be thus mentally "protected"? To say that would seem to be an admission that we are intellectually and morally unfit to play our part in what Justice Holmes has called the "experiment" of self-government. Have we, on that ground, abandoned or qualified the great experiment?

Here, then, is the question which we must try to answer as we interpret the First Amendment to the Constitution. In our discussions of public policy at home, do we intend that "dangerous" ideas shall be suppressed? Or are they, under the Constitution, guaranteed freedom from such suppression? And, correspondingly, in our dealings with other nations, are we saying to them, "The general welfare of the world requires that you and we shall not, in any way, abridge the freedom of expression and communication"? Or are we saying, "Every nation may, of course, forbid and punish the expression of ideas which are dangerous to the form of government or of industrial organization which it has established and is attempting to maintain"?

No one, of course, may prescribe that citizens of the United States shall interpret the Constitution in this way or that. It is not even required that the meaning of the Constitution shall be in the future what it has been in the past. We are free to change that meaning both by interpretation and by explicit amendment. But what is required of us by every consideration of honesty and self-respect is that we practice what we preach, that we preach only what we practice. What, then, as we deal with the present, as we plan for the future, do we intend that the principle of the freedom of speech shall mean?

CHAPTER I

THE RULERS AND THE RULED

THE PURPOSE of these lectures is to consider the freedom of speech which is guaranteed by the Constitution of the United States. The most general thesis of the argument is that, under the Constitution, there are two different freedoms of speech, and, hence, two different guarantees of freedom rather than only one.

More broadly, it may be asserted that our civil liberties, in general, are not all of one kind. They are of two kinds which, though radically different in constitutional status, are easily confused. And that confusion has been, and is, disastrous in its effect upon our understanding of the relations between an individual citizen and the government of the United States. The argument of these lectures is an attempt to clear away that confusion.

As an instance of the first kind of civil liberty I would offer that of religious or irreligious belief. In this country of ours, so far as the Constitution is effective, men are free to believe and to advocate or to disbelieve and to argue against, any creed. And the government is unqualifiedly forbidden to restrict that freedom. As an instance of the second kind, we may take the liberty of an individual to own, and to use the income from, his labor or his property. It is agreed among us that every man has a right, a liberty, to such ownership and use. And yet it is also agreed that the government may take whatever part of a man's income it deems necessary for the promoting of the general welfare. The liberty of owning and using property is, then, as contrasted with that of religious belief, a limited one. It may be invaded by the government. And the Constitution authorizes such invasion. It requires only that the procedure shall be properly and impartially carried out and that it shall be justified by public need.

Our Constitution, then, recognizes and protects two different sets of freedoms. One of these is open to restriction by the government. The other is not open to such restriction. It would be of great value to our argument and, in fact, to all attempts at political thinking in the United States, if there were available two sharply defined terms by which to identify these two fundamentally different kinds of civil liberty. But, alas, no such accurate use of words has been established among us. Men speak of the freedom of belief and the freedom of property as if, in the Constitution, the word "freedom," as used in these two cases, had the same meaning. Because of that confusion we are in constant danger of giving to a man's possessions the same dignity, the same status, as we give to the man himself. From that confusion our national life has suffered disastrous effects in all its phases. But for this disease of our minds there is, so far as I know, no specific semantic cure. All that we can do at present is to remember that such terms as liberty, freedom, civil rights, etc., are ambiguous. We must, then, in each specific case, try to keep clear what meaning we are using.

1

We Americans think of ourselves as politically free. We believe in self-government. If men are to be governed, we say, then that governing must be done, not by others, but by themselves. So far, therefore, as our own affairs are concerned, we refuse to submit to alien control. That refusal, if need be, we will carry to the point of rebellion, of revolution. And if other men, within the jurisdiction of our laws, are denied their right to political freedom, we will, in the same spirit, rise to their defense. Governments, we insist, derive their just powers from the consent of the governed. If that consent be lacking, governments have no just powers.

Now, this political program of ours, though passionately advocated by us, is not—as we all recognize—fully worked out in practice. Over one hundred and seventy years have gone by since the Declaration of Independence was written. But, to an unforgivable degree, citizens of the United States are still subjected to decisions in the making of which they have had no effective share. So far as that is true, we are not self-governed; we are not politically free. We are governed by others. And, perhaps worse, we are, without their consent, the governors of others.

But a more important point—which we Americans do not so readily recognize—is that of the intellectual difficulties which are inherent in the making and administering of this political program of ours. We do not see how baffling, even to the point of desperation, is the task of using our minds, to which we are summoned by our plan of government. That plan is not intellectually simple. Its victories are chiefly won, not by the carnage of battle, but by the sweat and agony of the mind. By contrast with it, the idea of alien government which we reject—whatever its other merits or defects—is easy to understand. It is suited to simple-minded people who are unwilling or unable to question their own convictions, who would defend their principles by suppressing that hostile criticism which is necessary for their clarification.

The intellectual difficulty of which I am speaking is sharply indicated by Professor Edward Hallett Carr, in his recent book, *The Soviet Impact on the Western World.* Mr. Carr tells us that our American political program, as we formulate it, is not merely unclear. It is essentially self-contradictory and hence, nonsensical. "Confusion of thought," he says, "is often caused by the habit common among politicians and writers of the English-speaking world, of defining democracy in formal and conventional terms as 'self-government' or 'government by consent.' " What these terms define, he continues, "is not democracy, but anarchy. Government of some kind is necessary in the common interest precisely because men will not govern themselves. 'Government by consent' is a contradiction in terms; for the purpose of government is to compel people to do what they would not do of their own volition. In short, government is a process by which some people exercise compulsion on others."[1]

Those words of Mr. Carr seem to me radically false. And, whatever else these lectures may do or fail to do, I hope that they may, in some measure, serve as a refutation of his contention. And yet the challenge of so able and well-balanced a mind cannot be ignored. If we believe in our principles we must make clear to others and to ourselves that self-government is not anarchy. We must show in what sense a free man, a free society, does practice self-direction. What, then, is the difference between a political system in which men do govern themselves and a political system in which men, without their consent, are governed by others? Unless we can make clear that distinction, discussion of freedom of speech or of any other freedom is meaningless and futile.

Alien government, we have said, is simple in idea. It is easy to understand. When one man or some self-chosen group holds control, without consent, over others, the relation between them is one of force and counterforce, of compulsion on the one hand and submission or resistance on the other. That relation is external and mechanical. It can be expressed in numbers—numbers of guns or planes or dollars or machines or policemen. The only basic fact is that one group "has the power" and the other group has not. In such a despotism, a ruler, by some excess of strength or guile or both, without the consent of his subjects, forces them into obedience. And in order to understand what he does, what they do, we need only measure the strength or weakness of the control and the strength or weakness of the resistance to it.

But government by consent—self-government—is not thus simple. It is, in fact, so complicated, so confusing, that, not only to the scholarly judgment of Mr. Carr, but also to the simple-mindedness which we call "shrewd, practical, calculating, common

[1] Edward Hallett Carr, *The Soviet Impact on the Western World* (New York, Macmillan, 1947), p. 10.

sense," it tends to seem silly, unrealistic, romantic, or—to use a favorite term of reproach—"idealistic." And the crux of the difficulty lies in the fact that, in such a society, the governors and the governed are not two distinct groups of persons. There is only one group—the self-governing people. Rulers and ruled are the same individuals. We, the People, are our own masters, our own subjects. But that inner relationship of men to themselves is utterly different in kind from the external relationship of one man to another. It cannot be expressed in terms of forces and compulsions. If we attempt to think about the political procedures of self-government by means of the ideas which are useful in describing the external control of a hammer over a nail or of a master over his slaves, the meaning slips through the fingers of our minds. For thinking which is done merely in terms of forces, political freedom does not exist.

At this point, a protest must be entered against the oversimplified advice which tells us that we should introduce into the realms of economics, politics, and morals the "methods" of the "sciences." Insofar as the advice suggests to us that we keep our beliefs within the limits of the evidence which warrants them, insofar as it tells us that our thinking about human relationships must be as exact and tentative, as orderly and inclusive, as is the work done by students of physical or biological fact, no one may challenge either its validity or its importance. To believe what one has no reason for believing is a crime of the first order. But, on the other hand, it must be urged that the chief source of our blundering ineptness in dealing with moral and political problems is that we do not know how to think about them except by quantitative methods which are borrowed from non-moral, non-political, non-social sciences. In this sense we need to be, not more scientific, but less scientific, not more quantitative but other than quantitative. We must create and use methods of inquiry, methods of belief which are suitable to the study of men as self-governing persons but not suitable to the study of forces or of machines. In the understanding of a free society, scientific thinking has an essential part to play. But it is a secondary part. We shall not understand the Constitution of the United States if we think of men only as pushed around by forces. We must see them also as governing themselves.

But the statement just made must be guarded against two easy misinterpretations. First, when we say that self-government is hard to interpret, we are not saying that it is mysterious or magical or irrational. Quite the contrary is true. No idea which we have is more sane, more matter-of-fact, more immediately sensible, than that of self-government. Whether it be in the field of individual or of social activity, men are not recognizable as men unless, in any given situation, they are using their minds to give direction to their behavior. But the point which we are making is that the externalized measuring of the play of forces which serves the purposes of business or of science is wholly unsuited to our dealing with problems of moral or political freedom. And we Americans seem characteristically blind to the distinction. We are at the top of the world in engineering. We are experts in the knowledge and manipulation of measurable forces, whether physical or psychological. We invent and run machines of ever new and amazing power and intricacy. And we are tempted by that achievement to see if we can manipulate men with the same skill and ingenuity. But the manipulataion of men is the destruction of self-government. Our skill, therefore, threatens our wisdom. In this respect the United States with its "know-how" is, today, the most dangerous nation in the world.

And, second, what we have said must not be allowed to obscure the fact that a free government, established by common consent, may and often must use force in compelling citizens to obey the laws. Every government, as such, must have external power. It must, in fact, be more powerful than any one of its citizens, than any group of them. Political freedom does not mean freedom from control. It means self-control. If, for example, a nation becomes involved in war, the government must decide who shall be drafted to leave his family and home, to risk his life, his health, his sanity, upon the battlefield. The government must also levy and collect and expend taxes. In general, it must determine how far and in what ways the customs and privileges of peace are to be swept aside. In all these cases it may be taken for granted that, in a self-governing society, minorities will disagree with the decisions which are made. May a minority man, then, by appeal to the principle of "consent," refuse to submit to military control? May he evade payment of taxes which he thinks unwise or unjust? May he say, "I did not approve of this measure; therefore, as a self-governing man, I claim the right to disobey it"?

Certainly not! At the bottom of every plan of self-government is a basic agreement, in which all the citizens have joined, that all matters of public policy shall be decided by corporate action, that such decisions shall be equally binding on all citizens, whether they agree with them or not, and that, if need be, they shall, by due legal procedure, be enforced upon anyone who refuses to conform to them. The man who rejects that agreement is not objecting to tyranny or despotism. He is objecting to political freedom. He is not a democrat. He is the anarchist of whom Mr. Carr speaks. Self-government is nonsense unless the "self" which governs is able and determined to make its will effective.

2

What, then, is this compact or agreement which underlies any plan for political freedom? It cannot be understood unless we distinguish sharply and persistently between the "submission" of a slave and the "consent" of a free citizen. In both cases it is agreed that obedience shall be required. Even when despotism is so extreme as to be practically indistinguishable from enslavement, a sort of pseudo consent is given by the subjects. When the ruling force is overwhelming, men are driven not only to submit, but also to agree to do so. For the time, at least, they decide to make the best of a bad situation rather than to struggle against hopeless odds. And, coordinate with this "submission" by the people, there are "concessions" by the ruler. For the avoiding of trouble, to establish his power, to manipulate one hostile force against another, he must take account of the desires and interests of his subjects, must manage to keep them from becoming too rebellious. The granting of such "concessions" and the accepting of them are, perhaps, the clearest evidence that a government is not democratic but is essentially despotic and alien.

But the "consent" of free citizens is radically different in kind from this "submission" of slaves. Free men talk about their government, not in terms of its "favors" but in terms of their "rights." They do not bargain. They reason. Every one of them is, of course, subject to the laws which are made. But if the Declaration of Independence means what it says, if we mean what it says, then no man is called upon to obey a law unless he himself, equally with his fellows, has shared in making it. Under an agreement to which, in the closing words of the Declaration of Independence, "we mutually pledge to each other our Lives, our Fortunes, and our sacred Honor," the consent which we give is not forced upon us. It expresses a voluntary compact among political equals. We, the People, acting together, either directly or through our representatives, make and administer law. We, the People, acting in groups or separately, are subject to the law. If we could make that double agreement effective, we would have accomplished the American Revolution. If we could understand that agreement we would understand the Revolution, which is still in the making. But the agreement can have meaning for us only as we clarify the tenuous and elusive distinction between a political "submission" which we abhor and a political "consent" in which we glory. Upon the effectiveness of that distinction rests the entire enormous and intricate structure of those free political institutions which we have pledged ourselves to build. If we can think that distinction clearly, we can be self-governing. If we lose our grip upon it, if, rightly or wrongly, we fall back into the prerevolutionary attitudes which regard our chosen representatives as alien and hostile to ourselves, nothing can save us from the slavery which, in 1776, we set out to destroy.

3

I have been saying that, under the plan of political freedom, we maintain by common consent a government which, being stronger than any one of us, than any group of us, can take control over all of us. But the word "control" strikes terror into the hearts of many "free" men, especially if they are mechanically minded about their freedom. Out of that fear there arises the passionate demand that the government which controls us must itself be controlled. By whom, and in what ways?

In abstract principle, that question is easy to answer. A government of free men can properly be controlled only by itself. Who else could be trusted by us to hold our political institutions in check? Shall any single individual or any special group be allowed to take domination over the agencies of control? There is only one situation in which free men can answer "yes" to that question. If the government, as an institution, has broken down, if the basic agreement has collapsed, then both the right and the duty of rebellion are thrust upon the individual citizens. In that chaotic and desperate situation they must, for the sake of a new order, revolt and destroy, as the American colonies in 1776 revolted and destroyed. But, short of such violent lawlessness in the interest of a new law, there can be no doubt that a free government must be its own master. If We, the People are to be controlled, then We, the People must do the controlling. As a corporate body, we must exercise control over our separate members. That principle is a flat denial of the suggestion that we, acting as an unorganized and irresponsible mob, may drive into submission ourselves acting as an organized government. What it means is that the body politic, organized as a nation, must recognize its own limitations of wisdom and of temper and of circumstance, and must, therefore, make adequate provision for self-criticism and self-restraint. The government itself must limit the government, must determine what it may and may not do. It must make sure that its attempts to make men free do not result in making them slaves.

Our own American constitutional procedure gives striking illustration of the double principle that no free government can submit to control other than its own and that, therefore, it must limit and control itself. For example, our agencies of government do their work under a scheme of mutual checks and balances. The Bill of Rights, also, sharply and explicitly defines boundaries beyond which acts of governing may not go. "Congress shall make no law . . ." it says. And again, "No person shall be held to answer for a capital or otherwise infamous crime unless . . ." And again, "Excessive bail shall not be required, nor excessive fines imposed, nor cruel and unusual punishments inflicted." All these and many other limits are set to the powers of government. But in every case—let it be noted—these limits are set by government. These enactments were duly proposed, discussed, adopted, interpreted, and enforced by regular political procedure. And, as the years have gone by, We, the People, who, by explicit compact, are the government, have maintained and interpreted and extended them. In some cases, we have reinterpreted them or have even abolished them. They are expressions of our own corporate self-control. They tell us that, by compact, explicit or implicit, we are self-governed.

Here, then, is the thesis upon which the argument of these lectures is to rest. At the bottom of our American plan of government there is, as Thomas Jefferson has firmly told us, a "compact." To Jefferson it is clear that as fellow citizens we have made and are continually remaking an agreement with one another, and that, whatever the cost, we are in honor bound to keep that agreement. The nature of the compact to which we "consent" is suggested by the familiar story of the meeting of the Pilgrims in the cabin of the Mayflower. "We whose names are underwritten, . . ." they said, ". . . Do by these Presents solemnly and mutually, in the presence of God, and one another, Covenant and Combine ourselves together into a Civil Body Politick, for our better ordering and preservation, and furtherance of the ends aforesaid; and by virtue hereof do enact, constitute, and frame such just and equal Laws, Ordinances, Acts, Constitutions, and Offices, from time to time, as shall be thought most meet and convenient for the general good of the Colony; unto which we promise all due submission and obedience. . . ." This is the same pledge of comradeship, of responsible cooperation in a joint undertaking, which was given in the concluding words of the Declaration of Independence already quoted—"We mutually pledge to each other our Lives, our Fortunes, and our sacred Honor." And, some years later, as the national revolution moved on from its first step to its second, from the negative task of destroying alien government to the positive work of creating self-government, the Preamble of the Constitution announced the common purposes in the pursuit of which we had become united. "We, the People of the United States," it says, "in order to form a more perfect Union, establish justice, insure domestic tranquillity, provide for the common defense, promote the general welfare, and secure the blessings of liberty to ourselves and our posterity, do ordain and establish this Constitution of the United States of America."

In those words it is agreed, and with every passing moment it is reagreed, that the people of the United States shall be self-governed. To that fundamental enactment all other provisions of the Constitution, all statutes, all administrative decrees, are subsidiary and dependent. All other purposes, whether individual or social, can find their legitimate scope and meaning only as they conform to the one basic purpose that the citizens of this nation shall make and shall obey their own laws, shall be at once their own subjects and their own masters.

Our preliminary remarks about the Constitution of the United States may, then, be briefly summarized. That Constitution is based upon a twofold political agreement. It is ordained that all

authority to exercise control, to determine common action, belongs to "We, the People." We, and we alone, are the rulers. But
it is ordained also that We, the People, are, all alike, subject to
control. Every one of us may be told what he is allowed to do,
what he is not allowed to do, what he is required to do. But this
agreed-upon requirement of obedience does not transform a ruler
into a slave. Citizens do not become puppets of the state when,
having created it by common consent, they pledge allegiance to
it and keep their pledge. Control by a self-governing nation is
utterly different in kind from control by an irresponsible despotism. And to confuse these two is to lose all understanding of what
political freedom is. Under actual conditions, there is no freedom
for men except by the authority of government. Free men are
not non-governed. They are governed—by themselves.

And now, after this long introduction, we are, I hope, ready
for the task of interpreting the First Amendment to the Constitution, of trying to clear away the confusions by which its
meaning has been obscured and even lost.

4

"Congress shall make no law . . . abridging the freedom of
speech . . ." says the First Amendment to the Constitution. As
we turn now to the interpreting of those words, three preliminary
remarks should be made.

First, let it be noted that, by those words, Congress is not debarred from all action upon freedom of speech. Legislation which
abridges that freedom is forbidden, but not legislation to enlarge
and enrich it. The freedom of mind which befits the members of
a self-governing society is not a given and fixed part of human
nature. It can be increased and established by learning, by teaching, by the unhindered flow of accurate information, by giving
men health and vigor and security, by bringing them together
in activities of communication and mutual understanding. And
the federal legislature is not forbidden to engage in that positive

enterprise of cultivating the general intelligence upon which the success of self-government so obviously depends. On the contrary, in that positive field the Congress of the United States has a heavy and basic responsibility to promote the freedom of speech.

And second, no one who reads with care the text of the First Amendment can fail to be startled by its absoluteness. The phrase, "Congress shall make no law . . . abridging the freedom of speech," is unqualified. It admits of no exceptions. To say that no laws of a given type shall be made means that no laws of that type shall, under any circumstances, be made. That prohibition holds good in war as in peace, in danger as in security. The men who adopted the Bill of Rights were not ignorant of the necessities of war or of national danger. It would, in fact, be nearer to the truth to say that it was exactly those necessities which they had in mind as they planned to defend freedom of discussion against them. Out of their own bitter experience they knew how terror and hatred, how war and strife, can drive men into acts of unreasoning suppression. They planned, therefore, both for the peace which they desired and for the wars which they feared. And in both cases they established an absolute, unqualified prohibition of the abridgment of the freedom of speech. That same requirement, for the same reasons, under the same Constitution, holds good today.

Against what has just been said it will be answered that twentieth-century America does not accept "absolutes" so readily as did the eighteenth century. But to this we must reply that the issue here involved cannot be dealt with by such twentieth-century a priori reasoning. It requires careful examination of the structure and functioning of our political system as a whole to see what part the principle of the freedom of speech plays, here and now, in that system. And when that examination is made, it seems to me clear that for our day and generation, the words of the First Amendment mean literally what they say. And what they say is that under no circumstances shall the freedom of speech be abridged. Whether or not that opinion can be justified is the primary issue with which this argument tries to deal.

But, third, this dictum which we rightly take to express the most vital wisdom which men have won in their striving for political freedom is yet—it must be admitted—strangely paradoxical. No one can doubt that, in any well-governed society, the legislature has both the right and the duty to prohibit certain forms of speech. Libellous assertions may be, and must be, forbidden and punished. So too must slander. Words which incite men to crime are themselves criminal and must be dealt with as such. Sedition and treason may be expressed by speech or writing.* And, in those cases, decisive repressive action by the government is imperative for the sake of the general welfare. All these necessities that speech be limited are recognized and provided for under the Constitution. They were not unknown to the writers of the First Amendment. That amendment, then, we may take it for granted, *does not forbid the abridging of speech.* But, at the same time, *it does forbid the abridging of the freedom of speech.* It is to the solving of that paradox, that apparent self-contradiction, that we are summoned if, as free men, we wish to know what the right of freedom of speech is.

5

As we proceed now to reflect upon the relations of a thinking and speaking individual to the government which guards his freedom, we may do well to turn back for a few moments to the analysis of those relations given by Plato. The Athenian philosopher of the fourth century B.C. was himself caught in our paradox. He saw the connection between self-government and

---

* I shall be grateful if the reader will eliminate from the sentence, "Sedition and treason may be expressed by speech or writing," the words "Sedition and." "Treason" is a genuine word, with an honest and carefully defined procedural meaning. But "sedition," as applied to belief or communication, is, for the most part, a tricky and misleading word. It is used chiefly to suggest that a "treasonable" crime has been committed in an area in which, under the Constitution, no such crime can exist. (Note added 1960.)

intelligence with a clarity and wisdom and wit which have never been excelled. In his two short dialogues, the *Apology* and the *Crito,* he grapples with the problem which we are facing.

In both dialogues, Plato is considering the right which a government has to demand obedience from its citizens. And in both dialogues, Socrates, a thinker and teacher who had aroused Plato from dogmatic slumber, is the citizen whose relations are discussed. The question is whether or not Socrates is in duty bound to obey the government. In the *Apology* the answer is "No." In the *Crito* the answer is "Yes." Plato is obviously using one of the favorite devices of the teacher. He is seeming to contradict himself. He is thereby demanding of his pupils that they save themselves and him from contradiction by making clear a basic and elusive distinction.

In the *Apology,* Socrates is on trial for his life. The charge against him is that in his teaching he has "corrupted the youth" and has "denied the Gods." On the evidence presented by a kind of un-Athenian Subversive Activities Committee he is found guilty. His judges do not wish to put him to death, but they warn him that, unless he will agree to stop his teaching or to change its tenor, they must order his execution. And to this demand for obedience to a decree abridging his freedom of speech, Socrates replies with a flat and unequivocal declaration of disobedient independence. My teaching, he says, is not, in that sense, under the abridging control of the government. Athens is a free city. No official, no judge, he declares, may tell me what I shall, or shall not, teach or think. He recognizes that the government has the power and the legal right to put him to death. But so far as the content of his teaching is concerned, he claims unqualified independence. "Congress shall make no law abridging the freedom of speech," he seems to be saying. Present-day Americans who wish to understand the meaning, the human intention, expressed by the First Amendment, would do well to read and to ponder again Plato's *Apology,* written in Athens twenty-four centuries ago. It may well be argued that if the *Apology* had not been written—by Plato or by someone else—the First Amendment would not have been written. The relation here is one of trunk and branch.

But the argument of the *Crito* seems, at least, to contradict that of the *Apology*. Here Socrates, having been condemned to death, is in prison awaiting the carrying out of the sentence. His friend Crito urges him to escape, to evade the punishment. This he refuses to do. He has no right, he says, to disobey the decision of the government that he must drink the hemlock. That government has legal authority over the life and death of its citizens. Even though it is mistaken, and, therefore, unjust, they must, in this field, conform to its decisions. For Socrates, obedience to the laws which would abridge his life is here quite as imperative as was disobedience to laws which would abridge his belief and the expression of it. In passages of amazing beauty and insight, Socrates explains that duty to Crito. He represents himself as conversing with The Laws of Athens about the compact into which they and he have entered. The Laws, he says, remind him that for seventy years, he has "consented" to them, has accepted from them all the rights and privileges of an Athenian citizen. Will he now, they ask, because his own life is threatened, withdraw his consent, annul the compact? To do that would be a shameful thing, unworthy of a citizen of Athens.

Plato is too great a teacher to formulate for us, or for his more immediate pupils, the distinction which he is here drawing. He demands of us that we make it for ourselves. But that there is a distinction and that the understanding of it is essential for the practice of freedom, he asserts passionately and without equivocation. If the government attempts to limit the freedom of a man's opinions, he tells us, that man, and his fellows with him, has both the right and the duty of disobedience. But if, on the other hand, by regular legal procedure, his life or his property is required of him, he must submit; he must let them go willingly. In one phase of man's activities, the government may exercise control over him. In another phase, it may not. What,

then, are those two phases? Only as we see clearly the distinction
between them, Plato is saying, do we know what government by
consent of the governed means.

6

The difficulties of the paradox of freedom as applied to speech
may perhaps be lessened if we now examine the procedure of the
traditional American town meeting. That institution is commonly, and rightly, regarded as a model by which free political
procedures may be measured. It is self-government in its simplest,
most obvious form.

In the town meeting the people of a community assemble to
discuss and to act upon matters of public interest—roads, schools,
poorhouses, health, external defense, and the like. Every man is
free to come. They meet as political equals. Each has a right and
a duty to think his own thoughts, to express them, and to listen
to the arguments of others. The basic principle is that the freedom of speech shall be unabridged. And yet the meeting cannot
even be opened unless, by common consent, speech is abridged.
A chairman or moderator is, or has been, chosen. He "calls the
meeting to order." And the hush which follows that call is a
clear indication that restrictions upon speech have been set up.
The moderator assumes, or arranges, that in the conduct of the
business, certain rules of order will be observed. Except as he is
overruled by the meeting as a whole, he will enforce those rules.
His business on its negative side is to abridge speech. For example, it is usually agreed that no one shall speak unless "recognized by the chair." Also, debaters must confine their remarks
to "the question before the house." If one man "has the floor,"
no one else may interrupt him except as provided by the rules.
The meeting has assembled, not primarily to talk, but primarily
by means of talking to get business done. And the talking must
be regulated and abridged as the doing of the business under
actual conditions may require. If a speaker wanders from the

point at issue, if he is abusive or in other ways threatens to defeat the purpose of the meeting, he may be and should be declared "out of order." He must then stop speaking, at least in that way. And if he persists in breaking the rules, he may be "denied the floor" or, in the last resort, "thrown out" of the meeting. The town meeting, as it seeks for freedom of public discussion of public problems, would be wholly ineffectual unless speech were thus abridged. It is not a Hyde Park. It is a parliament or congress. It is a group of free and equal men, cooperating in a common enterprise, and using for that enterprise responsible and regulated discussion. It is not a dialectical free-for-all. It is self-government.

These speech-abridging activities of the town meeting indicate what the First Amendment to the Constitution does not forbid. When self-governing men demand freedom of speech they are not saying that every individual has an unalienable right to speak whenever, wherever, however he chooses. They do not declare that any man may talk as he pleases, when he pleases, about what he pleases, about whom he pleases, to whom he pleases. The common sense of any reasonable society would deny the existence of that unqualified right. No one, for example, may, without consent of nurse or doctor, rise up in a sickroom to argue for his principles or his candidate. In the sickroom, that question is not "before the house." The discussion is, therefore, "out of order." To you who now listen to my words, it is allowable to differ with me, but it is not allowable for you to state that difference in words until I have finished my reading. Anyone who would thus irresponsibly interrupt the activities of a lecture, a hospital, a concert hall, a church, a machine shop, a classroom, a football field, or a home, does not thereby exhibit his freedom. Rather, he shows himself to be a boor, a public nuisance, who must be abated, by force if necessary.

What, then, does the First Amendment forbid? Here again the town meeting suggests an answer. That meeting is called to discuss and, on the basis of such discussion, to decide matters of public policy. For example, shall there be a school? Where shall it be located? Who shall teach? What shall be taught? The community has agreed that such questions as these shall be freely discussed and that, when the discussion is ended, decision upon them will be made by vote of the citizens. Now, in that method of political self-government, the point of ultimate interest is not the words of the speakers, but the minds of the hearers. The final aim of the meeting is the voting of wise decisions. The voters, therefore, must be made as wise as possible. The welfare of the community requires that those who decide issues shall understand them. They must know what they are voting about. And this, in turn, requires that so far as time allows, all facts and interests relevant to the problem shall be fully and fairly presented to the meeting. Both facts and interests must be given in such a way that all the alternative lines of action can be wisely measured in relation to one another. As the self-governing community seeks, by the method of voting, to gain wisdom in action, it can find it only in the minds of its individual citizens. If they fail, it fails. That is why freedom of discussion for those minds may not be abridged.

The First Amendment, then, is not the guardian of unregulated talkativeness. It does not require that, on every occasion, every citizen shall take part in public debate. Nor can it even give assurance that everyone shall have opportunity to do so. If, for example, at a town meeting, twenty like-minded citizens have become a "party," and if one of them has read to the meeting an argument which they have all approved, it would be ludicrously out of order for each of the others to insist on reading it again. No competent moderator would tolerate that wasting of the time available for free discussion. What is essential is not that everyone shall speak, but that everything worth saying shall be said. To this end, for example, it may be arranged that each of the known conflicting points of view shall have, and shall be limited to, an assigned share of the time available. But however it be arranged, the vital point, as stated negatively, is that no suggestion of policy shall be denied a hearing because it is on one side of the issue rather than another. And this means that though citizens may, on other grounds, be barred from speaking, they may not be barred because their views are thought to be false or dangerous. No plan of action shall be outlawed because someone in control thinks it unwise, unfair, un-American. No speaker may be declared "out of order" because we disagree with what he intends to say. And the reason for this equality of status in the field of ideas lies deep in the very foundations of the self-governing process. When men govern themselves, it is they—and no one else—who must pass judgment upon un-wisdom and unfairness and danger. And that means that unwise ideas must have a hearing as well as wise ones, unfair as well as fair, dangerous as well as safe, un-American as well as American. Just so far as, at any point, the citizens who are to decide an issue are denied acquaintance with information or opinion or doubt or disbelief or criticism which is relevant to that issue, just so far the result must be ill-considered, ill-balanced planning for the general good. *It is that mutilation of the thinking process of the community against which the First Amendment to the Constitution is directed.* The principle of the freedom of speech springs from the necessities of the program of self-government. It is not a Law of Nature or of Reason in the abstract. It is a deduction from the basic American agreement that public issues shall be decided by universal suffrage.

If, then, on any occasion in the United States it is allowable to say that the Constitution is a good document it is equally allowable, in that situation, to say that the Constitution is a bad document. If a public building may be used in which to say, in time of war, that the war is justified, then the same building may be used in which to say that it is not justified. If it be publicly argued that conscription for armed service is moral and necessary, it may likewise be publicly argued that it is immoral and unnecessary. If it may be said that American political institutions are superior to those of England or Russia or Germany, it may, with equal freedom, be said that those of England or Russia or Germany are superior to ours. These conflicting views may be expressed, must be expressed, not because they are valid, but because they are relevant. If they are responsibly entertained by anyone, we, the voters, need to hear them. When a question of policy is "before the house," free men choose to meet it not with their eyes shut, but with their eyes open. To be afraid of ideas, any idea, is to be unfit for self-government. Any such suppression of ideas about the common good, the First Amendment condemns with its absolute disapproval. The freedom of ideas shall not be abridged.

CHAPTER II

CLEAR AND PRESENT DANGER

IN OUR first lecture we found the political program of self-government to be bewildering and paradoxical. The principles of our Constitution are not, I think, contradictory of each other. And yet they are certainly beset, if not by contradiction, at least by the appearance of it. What do we Americans mean when we say that one hundred and forty million people, acting together as a body politic, are pledged to take legislative, executive, and judicial control over those same one hundred and forty million people, acting separately as individuals and as groups? And, especially, what do we mean when we say that men who thus become self-governed are thereby made politically free? As we try to understand this program of ours, the strain upon our thinking apparatus seems almost unbearable. It is little wonder that we have difficulty in explaining our institutions to other peoples, and even more difficulty when, after conquering another nation in war and taking domination over it, we proceed to impose upon it our own plan of free self-government. The plain truth is that, if the Constitution be taken as the test of Americanism, our current methods of political thinking are curiously un-American. Our minds, as at present educated, are not equipped for the work they have to do. It is in the midst of that confusion, that mental unpreparedness, that we must attempt to fight our way toward an understanding of the meaning of the First Amendment of our Constitution.

Now the primary purpose of this lecture is to challenge the interpretation of the freedom-of-speech principle which, since

1919, has been adopted by the Supreme Court of the United States. In that year, and in the years which have ensued, the court, following the lead of Justice Oliver Wendell Holmes, has persistently ruled that the freedom of speech of the American community may constitutionally be abridged by legislative action. That ruling annuls the most significant purpose of the First Amendment. It destroys the intellectual basis of our plan of self-government. The court has interpreted the dictum that Congress shall not abridge the freedom of speech by defining the conditions under which such abridging is allowable. Congress, we are now told, is forbidden to destroy our freedom except when it finds it advisable to do so.

The 1919 decision of which I am speaking arose from a review by the Supreme Court of the conviction, during World War I, of a group of persons who were accused of obstructing the drafting of men into the army. In the course of the trial in the lower court it had been shown that the defendants had mailed circulars to men who had been passed by the exemption boards. These circulars contained violent denunciations of the Conscription Act under which the draft was being administered. They impressed upon their readers "the right to assert your opposition to the draft," and urged the draftees to exercise that right. The Supreme Court unanimously sustained the conviction and Mr. Holmes wrote the opinion. In doing so, he formulated a new test of the freedom of speech guarantee. During the twenty-eight years which have passed since that decision was handed down, that test in varying forms has been accepted as expressing the law of the land. It is known as the principle of "clear and present danger."

The words in which Mr. Holmes explained and justified his decision have often been quoted. "We admit," he said, "that in many places and in ordinary times, the defendants in saying all that was said in the circular, would have been within their constitutional rights. But the character of every act depends upon the circumstances in which it is done. The most stringent protection of free speech would not protect a man in falsely shouting fire in a theatre, and causing a panic. It does not even protect a man from an injunction against uttering words which may have all the effect of force. . . . The question in every case is whether the words used are used in such circumstances and are of such a nature as to create a clear and present danger that they will bring about the substantive evils that Congress has a right to prevent. It is a question of proximity and degree. When a nation is at war many things that might be said in time of peace are such a hindrance to its effort that their utterance will not be endured so long as men fight, and that no court could regard them as protected by any constitutional right. It seems to be admitted that, if an actual obstruction of the recruiting service were proved, liability for words that produced that effect might be enforced."[2]

The epoch-making importance of that argument is beyond question. Professor Zechariah Chafee, Jr., one of our most thoughtful and persistent students of free speech, says of it, "The concept of freedom received for the first time an authoritative judicial interpretation in accordance with the purposes of the framers of the Constitution."[3] As the sequel will show, we may, perhaps, differ from Mr. Chafee as to the success of Mr. Holmes in interpreting the purposes of the makers of the First Amendment. The formula offers an exception to the principle rather than an interpretation of it. But no one can doubt his judgment of the significance and the novelty of the argument which Mr. Holmes devised. That argument may or may not be valid. But, valid or not, it has striking originality and it has been widely and deeply influential.

As we proceed, in the remaining lectures of this series, to examine and perhaps to reject the attitude toward the freedom of

---

[2] 249 U.S. 47. Zechariah Chafee, Jr., *Free Speech in the United States* (Cambridge, Mass., Harvard University Press, 1942), p. 81.

[3] Chafee, *op. cit.*, p. 82.

speech which Mr. Holmes has defined, two explanatory remarks seem necessary.

First, as already noted, we shall criticize the decision of the Supreme Court, not after the manner of lawyers, but from the point of view of a teacher. In the American schools and colleges, thousands of men and women are devoting their lives to the attempt to lead their pupils into active and intelligent sharing in the activities of self-government. And to us who labor at that task of educating Americans it becomes, year by year, more evident that the Supreme Court has a large part to play in our national teaching. That court is commissioned to interpret to us our own purposes, our own meanings. To a self-governing community it must make clear what, in actual practice, self-governing is. And its teaching has peculiar importance because it interprets principles of fact and of value, not merely in the abstract, but also in their bearing upon the concrete, immediate problems which are, at any given moment, puzzling and dividing us. But it is just those problems with which any vital system of education is concerned. And for this reason, the court holds a unique place in the cultivating of our national intelligence. Other institutions may be more direct in their teaching influence. But no other institution is more deeply decisive in its effect upon our understanding of ourselves and our government.

But, second, the Supreme Court, like any other teacher, may be wrong as well as right, may do harm as well as good. There is, it is true, a sense in which the court is always right. As Chief Justice Hughes is said to have remarked in the days when he was Governor of the State of New York: "We are under a Constitution; but the Constitution is what the courts say it is." Now, for the purposes of action at a given time, that dictum is clearly true. When opinions differ as to what the Constitution or the statutes mean, some court must decide among them, and, in one sense, we must accept its judgment. But it is equally true, and perhaps more important, to say that the law is what the Supreme Court, more or less successfully, is trying to say. Or, even better, the law is what that court ought to say. As they study their cases, the members of the Supreme Court are not merely trying to discover what they are going to say. They are trying to decide what, in that situation, it is right to say in fact and principle. And as they grapple with that problem, they are keenly aware of their difficulties, of their lack of success. The individual members recognize frankly their own fallibilities, as well as those of their brethren. They are often puzzled and uncertain. They hand down opposing opinions. From time to time, their judgments are reconsidered and changed. Granted, then, that on any specific occasion we must, as Mr. Hughes suggests, "abide by" the rulings of the court; it does not follow that we must "agree with" them. Our duty, as free men, to reflect upon judicial pronouncements is quite as imperative as our duty to submit to their temporary legal authority. Not even our wisest interpreters, those whom we trust most, can give us final dogmas about self-government. They and we together must still be thinking about what freedom is and how it works.

And, in the problem before us—that of the First Amendment —as we gather up the import of a series of opinions and decisions in which, since 1919, the phrase, "clear and present danger," has held a dominating influence, I wish to argue that their effect upon our understanding of self-government has been one of disaster. The philosophizing of Mr. Holmes has, I think, led us astray. As already remarked, it has, in effect, led to the annulment of the First Amendment rather than to its interpretation. And since, among all the provisions of the Constitution, those which protect intellectual freedom come nearest to the work of the teacher, it is in the field of education that such an error may be most clearly seen, its consequences most keenly felt. In the interest of American education, therefore, I ask you to plunge with me into a criticism of that interpretation of the freedom of speech which, since 1919, the Supreme Court has presented to the people of our country, to whom, as an interpreter, it is responsible.

1

In the opinion from which we have quoted, Mr. Holmes formulates and answers, in part at least, the question with which any interpretation of the freedom of speech must try to deal. And, as he does so, his words have the disturbing and provocative quality of first-rate dialectical teaching. He had a talent for challenging the slothfulness, the contentment, of the inactive mind. Speaking to us as the interpreter of our own intentions, he tells us that certain forms of utterance "will not be endured" by us. But how do those forms of speech differ from those others which will be endured, which we welcome and approve as playing a proper and necessary part in the life of the community? What is the line, the principle, which marks off those speech activities which are liable to legislative abridgment from those which, under the Constitution, the legislature is forbidden to regulate or to suppress? Here is the critical question which must be studied, not only by the Supreme Court, but by every American who wishes to meet the intellectual responsibilities of his citizenship.

As we proceed now to grapple with this basic problem, it is at once evident that we cannot understand either the First Amendment or the "clear and present danger" interpretation of it unless we take into consideration certain other provisions of the Constitution which, more or less directly, are concerned with the freedom of speech. Three of these seem especially important.

First, we must remember that, in the Constitution as it stood before it was amended by the Bill of Rights, the principle of the freedom of public discussion had been already clearly recognized and adopted. Article I, section 6, of the Constitution, as it defines the duties and privileges of the members of Congress, says, ". . . and for any speech or debate in either House, they shall not be questioned in any other place." Here is a prohibition against abridgment of the freedom of speech which is equally uncompromising, equally absolute, with that of the First Amendment. Unqualifiedly, the freedom of debate of our representatives upon the floor of either house is protected from abridging interference. May that protection, under the Constitution, be limited or withdrawn in time of clear and present danger? And if not, why not?

No one can possibly doubt or deny that congressional debate, on occasion, brings serious and immediate threat to the general welfare. For example, military conscription, both in principle and in procedure, has been bitterly attacked by our federal representatives. On the floors of both houses, in time of peace as well as in war, national policies have been criticized with an effectiveness which the words of private citizens could never achieve. Shall we, then, as we guard against "substantive evils that we have a right to prevent," call our representatives to account in some other place? It is commonly believed, for example, that at the very time when Mr. Holmes was writing his opinion, certain "wilful men" in Congress were blocking President Wilson's plans for peace and were thereby doing enormous damage both to the nation and to the world. It is possible that, in large measure, they made World War II inevitable. But they were never brought to trial for that dreadful offense. Their liability for words that obstructed the organization of the world for peace was never enforced by legal action. And the reason is clear. If congressional immunity were not absolute and unconditional, the whole program of representative self-government would be broken down. And likewise, by common consent, the same kind of immunity is guaranteed to the judges in our courts. Everyone knows that the dissenting opinions of members of the Supreme Court are a clear and present threat to the effectiveness of majority decisions. And yet the freedom of the minorities on the bench to challenge and to dissent has not been legally abridged. Nor will it be.

And that fact throws strong and direct light upon the provision of the First Amendment that the public discussions of "citizens" shall have the same immunity. In the last resort, it is not our representatives who govern us. We govern ourselves, using them. And we do so in such ways as our own free judgment may decide. And, that being true, it is essential that when we speak in the open forum, we "shall not be questioned in any other place." It is not enough for us, as self-governing men, that we be governed wisely and justly, by someone else. We insist on doing our own governing. The freedom which we grant to our representatives is merely a derivative of the prior freedom which belongs to us as voters. In spite of all the dangers which it involves, Article I, section 6, suggests that the First Amendment means what it says: In the field of common action, of public discussion, the freedom of speech shall not be abridged.

And, second, the Fifth Amendment—by contrast of meaning, rather than by similarity—throws light upon the First. By the relevant clause of the Fifth Amendment we are told that no person within the jurisdiction of the laws of the United States may be "deprived of life, liberty, or property, without due process of law." And, whatever may have been the original reference of the term "liberty," as used in that sentence when it was written, it has been, in recent times, construed by the Supreme Court to include "the liberty of speech." The Fifth Amendment is, then, saying that the people of the United States have a civil liberty of speech which, by due legal process, the government may limit or suppress. But this means that, under the Bill of Rights, there are two freedoms, or liberties, of speech, rather than only one. There is a "freedom of speech" which the First Amendment declares to be non-abridgable. But there is also a "liberty of speech" which the Fifth Amendment declares to be abridgable. And for the inquiry in which we are engaged, the distinction between these two, the fact that there are two, is of fundamental importance. The Fifth Amendment, it appears, has to do with a class of utterances concerning which the legislature may, legitimately, raise the question, "Shall they be endured?" The First Amendment, on the other hand, has to do with a class of utterances concerning which that question may never legitimately be raised. And if that be true, then the problem which Mr. Holmes has suggested—that of separating two classes of utterances—becomes the problem of defining the difference between, and the relation between, the First and Fifth amendments, so far as they deal with matters of speech.

The nature of this difference comes to light if we note that the "liberty" of speech which is subject to abridgment is correlated, in the Fifth Amendment, with our rights to "life" and "property." These are private rights. They are individual possessions. And there can be no doubt that among the many forms of individual action and possession which are protected by the Constitution—not from regulation, but from undue regulation—the right to speak one's mind as one chooses is esteemed by us as one of our most highly cherished private possessions. Individuals have, then, a private right of speech which may on occasion be denied or limited, though such limitations may not be imposed unnecessarily or unequally. So says the Fifth Amendment. But this limited guarantee of the freedom of a man's wish to speak is radically different in intent from the unlimited guarantee of the freedom of public discussion, which is given by the First Amendment. The latter, correlating the freedom of speech in which it is interested with the freedom of religion, of press, of assembly, of petition for redress of grievances, places all these alike beyond the reach of legislative limitation, beyond even the due process of law. With regard to them, Congress has no negative powers whatever. There are, then, in the theory of the Constitution, two radically different kinds of utterances. The constitutional status of a merchant advertising his wares, of a paid lobbyist fighting for the advantage of his client, is utterly different from that of a citizen who is planning for the general welfare. And from this it follows that the Constitution provides differently for two different kinds of "freedom of speech."

Now, the basic error which we shall find in the "clear and present danger" principle, as it seeks to separate speech which will be endured from speech which will not be endured, is that it ignores or denies this difference of reference between the First and Fifth amendments. Mr. Holmes and the Supreme Court have ventured to annul the First Amendment because they have believed that the due process clause of the Fifth Amendment could take its place. But if that substitution can be shown to be invalid; if, under the Constitution, we have two essentially different freedoms of speech rather than only one, the position taken by the court becomes untenable. Here, then, is the crucial issue of our argument. Does the Bill of Rights protect two different freedoms of speech, or only one? To that issue we must return when the argument of Mr. Holmes has been more adequately stated.

A third provision of the Constitution which we must consider is found in the final words of the First Amendment itself. It is significant as showing how curiously intermingled are public and private interests, as the government is called upon to deal with them. The words in question give to petitions for redress of grievances the same absolute guarantee of freedom which is granted to religion, speech, press, and assembly. With none of these may Congress interfere. But a petition for redress of grievance seems, on the face of it, to express private interest. Why, then, is it given the unlimited freedom of the First Amendment? The answer is, I think, that such a petition, whatever its motivation, raises definitely a question of public policy. It asserts an error in public decision. The petitioners have found, or think they have found, that in the adoption of a government policy, some private interest has been misjudged or overlooked. They ask, therefore, for reconsideration. And in doing so, they are clearly within the field of the public interest. They are not saying, "We want this; please give it to us." They are saying to officials who are their agents, "You have made a mistake; kindly correct it." And such a responsible statement that some interest has not been properly judged gives valid ground for a public demand for reconsideration. Because the freedom of that demand may not be abridged, it is guarded by the First Amendment.

2

Now, with these materials from the Constitution before us, we must return to Mr. Holmes and to the problem of separating by definition the abridgable and non-abridgable freedoms of speech. In the opinion from which we have quoted, Mr. Holmes brilliantly suggests one of the most popular answers to our problem. Speech, he tells us, is sometimes more than an expression of thought. It may be a form of action. The words in which Mr. Holmes makes this point are, perhaps, his best-known utterance.

"The most stringent protection of free speech," he says, "would not protect a man in *falsely*[4] shouting fire in a theatre, and causing a panic." Such a lie in such a situation is, in fact, a way of attempting murder. It attacks the lives of the persons in the theatre as directly and effectively as would the use of bludgeons or pistols or poison gas. It produces—to borrow another phrase from the same opinion, "substantive evils that Congress [or some other legal body] has a right to prevent." Such an utterance may, therefore, as a murderous act, be forbidden by statute. If any man is accused of disobeying that statute, justice requires that he be given a fair trial. But he is liable to trial. And if he is found guilty, he may be deprived of life, liberty, or property, by way of punishment. And as that legal procedure moves on, the First Amendment has nothing to say about it. The man who falsely shouted "fire" was not discussing the public interest, though the success of his maneuver depended on his pretending to do so. He was deliberately and falsely starting a dangerous panic. Speech-actions such as that are clearly within the field of private interest and, hence, of legislative abridgment.

Speech, then, may be action, Mr. Holmes tells us. And action which is criminal may be forbidden and punished. But what is the relevance of those facts for our problem of separating, in principle, speech which may be abridged from speech which may

---

[4] Italics mine. This word is too often ignored in the reading of the opinion.

not be abridged? Does it mean that whenever speech is an act, it has, therefore, no claim to the freedom guaranteed by the First Amendment? That suggestion is clearly absurd. The citizen who votes "Aye" or "No" on an issue of public policy has acted. The judge who condemns a man to fine or imprisonment or death, the Congress which declares war or the ending of war, the president who vetoes an act of Congress—all these are acting, in the same sense as did the man who shouted "fire." But the primary purpose of the First Amendment is the guaranteeing of freedom to just such speech-actions as these. Voters must vote freely. Judges must judge freely. Congress must enact freely. The president must "preside" freely. And in none of these cases may the freedom of the speech-act be abridged. The distinction between speech-actions and speech-thoughts is not, then, the distinction which we need for the proper interpretation of the First Amendment. The fire-shouting illustration given by Mr. Holmes tells us of one type of action, viz., criminal action, which is not protected by the principle of the freedom of speech. It does not follow, however, that all speech-acts are to be denied the freedom guaranteed by that principle.

Another popular solution of our problem, closely related to the first, is indicated by Mr. Holmes and is rightly rejected by him. It is the suggestion that speech which incites men to action is, as such, debarred from the protection of the First Amendment. It must, of course, be recognized that a person who successfully incites another to act must share in the legal responsibility for the consequences of the act. The man who effectively urges another to arson or theft may properly be dealt with as an arsonist or a thief. Shall we then say that no incitement to action —as contrasted with an expression of opinion—is entitled to the freedom of speech which the Constitution guarantees?

The responsibility for accepting or rejecting that theory was presented to Mr. Holmes when he dissented from a decision, written by Mr. Sanford, confirming the conviction of a Communist who had shared in the publication and distribution of a passionate left-wing manifesto. The manifesto in the case was a Communist call to battle. It declared, "The proletarian revolution and the Communist reconstruction of society—the struggle for these—is now indispensable . . . The Communist International calls the proletariat of the world to the final struggle." Speaking for the court, Mr. Sanford had found that these words have no claim to "liberty of expression." "This is not," he said, "the expression of philosophical abstraction, the mere prediction of future events, it is the language of direct incitement." And to this he adds, "The jury were justified in rejecting the view that it was a mere academic and harmless discussion of the advantages of communism and advanced socialism."[5]

Freedom to engage in "mere academic and harmless discussion"! Is that the freedom which is guarded by the First Amendment? Is that the cause for which the followers of Socrates have fought and died through the ages? As against that intolerable belittling of the practical value of human freedom of mind, Mr. Holmes, in his dissent, entered spirited, if not very coherent, words of protest. "It is said that this Manifesto was more than a theory, that it was an incitement. Every idea is an incitement. It offers itself for belief, and if believed, it is acted on unless some other belief outweighs it, or some failure of energy stifles the movement at its birth. The only difference between the expression of an opinion and an incitement in the narrower sense is the speaker's enthusiasm for the result. Eloquence may set fire to reason. But whatever may be thought of the redundant discourse before us, it had no chance of starting a present conflagration. If, in the long run, the beliefs expressed in proletarian dictatorship are destined to be accepted by the dominant forces of the community, the only meaning of free speech is that they should be given their chance and have their way."

What Mr. Holmes here says about opinions and incitements and their relations to one another may be challenged in many ways. Surely, opinions are often very enthusiastic. And, further,

5 268 U.S. 652.

incitements may be tentative and tepid and lacking in eloquence. Nor, if words are used in the senses relevant to our inquiry, can it be validly said that every idea is, legally, an incitement. But, however that may be, the magnificent words of the final sentence leave no doubt that, on the essential issue, the heart of Mr. Holmes is in the right place. He demands freedom not merely for idle contemplation, but for the vigorous thinking and deciding which determine public action. Human discourse, as the First Amendment sees it, is not "a mere academic and harmless discussion." If it were, the advocates of self-government would be as little concerned about it as they would be concerned about the freedom of men playing solitaire or chess. The First Amendment was not written primarily for the protection of those intellectual aristocrats who pursue knowledge solely for the fun of the game, whose search for truth expresses nothing more than a private intellectual curiosity or an equally private delight and pride in mental achievement. It was written to clear the way for thinking which serves the general welfare. It offers defense to men who plan and advocate and incite toward corporate action for the common good. On behalf of such men it tells us that every plan of action must have a hearing, every relevant idea of fact or value must have full consideration, whatever may be the dangers which that activity involves. It makes no difference whether a man is advocating conscription or opposing it, speaking in favor of a war or against it, defending democracy or attacking it, planning a communist reconstruction of our economy or criticising it. So long as his active words are those of participation in public discussion and public decision of matters of public policy, the freedom of those words may not be abridged. That freedom is the basic postulate of a society which is governed by the votes of its citizens.

"If, in the long run, the beliefs expressed in proletarian dictatorship are destined to be accepted by the dominant forces of the community, the only meaning of free speech is that they should be given their chance and have their way." That is Americanism. In these wretched days of postwar and, it may be, of prewar, hysterical brutality, when we Americans, from the president down, are seeking to thrust back Communist belief by jailing its advocates, by debarring them from office, by expelling them from the country, by hating them, the gallant, uncompromising words of Mr. Holmes, if we would listen to them, might help to restore our sanity, our understanding of the principles of the Constitution. They might arouse in us something of the sense of shame which the nation so sorely needs.

3

Mr. Holmes, then, rejects Mr. Sanford's doctrine that all incitements to action are properly barred from the protection of the First Amendment. But what principle of differentiation, as among incitements, does he put in its place? A partial answer to that question is given by the test of "clear and present danger." That test, as already noted, does not tell us in positive terms what forms of speech can rightly claim freedom, and on what ground they can claim it. But it does declare, on the negative side, that certain forms of speech, under the Constitution, are not entitled to freedom. For the elucidation of that statement we must turn back to the opinion in which the new test was first formulated.

In the course of his argument Mr. Holmes says, "The question in every case is whether the words used are used in such circumstances and are of such a nature as to create a clear and present danger that they will bring about the substantive evils that Congress has a right to prevent." And to this he adds, a few sentences later, "It seems to be admitted that, if an actual obstruction of the recruiting service were proved, liability for words that produced that effect might be enforced."

As one reads these words of Mr. Holmes, one is uneasily aware of the dangers of his rhetorical skill. At two points the argument seems at first much more convicing than it turns out to be. First, the phrase, "substantive evils that Congress has a right to prevent," seems to settle the issue by presumption, seems to establish the right of legislative control. If the legislature has both the right and the duty to prevent certain evils, then apparently it follows that the legislature must be authorized to take whatever action is needed for the preventing of those evils. But our plan of government by limited powers forbids that that inference be drawn. The Bill of Rights, for example, is a series of denials that the inference is valid. It lists, one after the other, forms of action which, however useful they might be in the service of the general welfare, the legislature is forbidden to take. And, that being true, the "right to prevent evils" does not give unqualifiedly the right to prevent evils. In the judgment of the Constitution, some preventions are more evil than are the evils from which they would save us. And the First Amendment is a case in point. If that amendment means anything, it means that certain substantive evils which, in principle, Congress has a right to prevent, must be endured if the only way of avoiding them is by the abridging of that freedom of speech upon which the entire structure of our free institutions rests.

And, again, in another way, the argument of Mr. Holmes tempts us into the accepting of a conclusion which is not justified by the evidence which is presented. In the case before the court, the defendants had been, in the opinion of Mr. Holmes, rightly convicted of criminal action, in the form of a deliberate obstruction of the draft in time of war. But the principle which Mr. Holmes formulates to justify that conviction is so broad that, under it, any utterance which threatens clear and present danger to the public safety, whether intended to impede the action of the government or not, may be suppressed and punished. No form of argument could have been more unfortunate than this. Taken literally, it means that in all "dangerous" situations, minorities, however law-abiding and loyal, must be silent. It puts upon them all alike, if they speak honestly, the stigma of criminal disloyalty.

The argument which accomplishes this transition needs careful watching. It moves in two steps. First, Mr. Holmes tells us, the defendants were accused of a criminal attack upon the safety of the country. And the evidence in support of that charge he finds to be adequate. "Of course," he says, "the document would not have been sent unless it had been intended to have some effect and we do not see what effect it could be expected to have upon persons subject to the draft except to obstruct the carrying of it out. The defendants do not deny that the jury might find against them on this point."

But, second, the "clear and present danger" argument, which Mr. Holmes here offers, moves quickly from deliberate obstruction of a law to reasonable protest against it. Taken as it stands, his formula tells us that whenever the expression of a minority opinion involves clear and present danger to the public safety it may be denied the protection of the First Amendment. And that means that whenever crucial and dangerous issues have come upon the nation, free and unhindered discussion of them must stop. If, for example, a majority in Congress is taking action against "substantive evils which Congress has a right to prevent," a minority which opposes such action is not entitled to the freedom of speech of Article I, section 6. Under that ruling, dissenting judges might, in "dangerous" situations, be forbidden to record their dissents. Minority citizens might, in like situations, be required to hold their peace. No one, of course, believes that this is what Mr. Holmes or the court intended to say. But it is what, in plain words, they did say. The "clear and present danger" opinion stands on the record of the court as a peculiarly inept and unsuccessful attempt to formulate an exception to the principle of the freedom of speech.

4

In support of this criticism it is worthy of note that, both by Mr. Holmes and by Mr. Brandeis who, in general, concurred with him, the "clear and present danger" formula was very quickly found to be unsatisfactory. Within the same year, 1919, in which the principle had found its first expression, these two gallant defenders of freedom were confronted by the fact that the great majority of their colleagues were taking very seriously the assertion of Mr. Holmes that whenever any utterance creates clear and present danger to the public safety, that utterance may be forbidden and punished. Against that doctrine, the two dissenters spoke out with insistent passion. It is not enough, they said, that a danger created by speech be clear and present. It must also be very serious. In this vein, Mr. Holmes, with the approval of Mr. Brandeis, wrote, "I think we should be eternally vigilant against attempts to check the expression of opinions that we loathe and think to be fraught with death, unless they so imminently threaten interference with the lawful and pressing purposes of the law that an immediate check is required to save the country."[6] If the modification here suggested had been made when the principle was first devised it could not possibly have been applied to the case then before the court. But in the ten years which followed, this additional test of the extreme gravity of the danger involved is so strongly urged by both justices that the basic meaning of the test is, for them, radically altered. By implication, at least, it becomes no longer recognizable as the principle of "clear and present danger." The danger must be clear and present, but, also, terrific.

The character of this change begins to appear when Mr. Brandeis, with Mr. Holmes agreeing, says, "The fact that speech is likely to result in some violence or destruction of property is not enough to justify its suppression. There must be probability of serious injury to the State."[7] And again, we read from the same source, "Moreover, even imminent danger cannot justify resort to prohibition of these functions essential to effective democracy, unless the evil apprehended is relatively serious. Pro-

[6] Abrams et al. v. U.S., 250 U.S. 616 (1919); Chafee, *op. cit.*, p. 137.
[7] Whitney v. California, 274 U.S. 352 (1927).

hibition of free speech and assembly is a measure so stringent that it would be inappropriate as the means for averting a relatively trivial harm to society."[8]

But the transformation of the principle does not stop with the addition of seriousness to clarity and immediacy. The more one reads the opinions of Mr. Holmes and Mr. Brandeis on questions of free speech in times of emergency, the more one becomes convinced that they are engaged in an attempt which James Stephens describes himself as making when he says:

> I would think until I found
> Something I can never find;
> Something lying on the ground,
> In the bottom of my mind.

In support of this suggestion may I note the fact that in the expositions of the formula of "clear and present danger," the most difficult and tantalizing factor for a reader has always been the insistence that a danger must be imminent, rather than remote, if it is to justify suppression. What is the basis for that insistence? It is relatively easy to understand why such a danger must be "clear." But why is it necessary that it be "present"? If the justification of suppression is, as Mr. Holmes says, that Congress is required and empowered to guard against dangers to the public safety, why should not that justification apply to clear and remote evils as well as to those which are clear and present? Surely we are not being told that, as Congress guards the common welfare, shortsightedness on its part is a virtue. Why, then, may it not take the same action in providing against the dangers of the future? As one reads the words of the advocates of the doctrine one feels certain that there is a valid reason for this differentiation which they are making. But in the early opinions, at least, that reason is never brought to light. The test remains, as Chief Justice Stone once described it, a "working device,"

[8] *Ibid.*

rather than a reasoned principle. It means something, but it does not succeed in saying what that meaning is.

Eight years after the first formulation of the doctrine, however, Mr. Brandeis, writing with the approval of Mr. Holmes, moved forward toward an explanation of this immediacy. But the logical effect of this change was to lead the way toward the substitution of a valid principle of freedom for that given in the "clear and present danger" test. "Those who won our independence by revolution," he says, "were not cowards. They did not fear political change. They did not exalt order at the cost of liberty. To courageous, self-reliant men, with confidence in the power of free and fearless reasoning applied through the processes of popular government, no danger flowing from speech can be deemed clear and present, unless the incidence of the evil apprehended is so imminent that it may befall before there is opportunity for free discussion. If there be time to expose through discussion the falsehood and fallacies, to avert the evil by the processes of education, the remedy to be applied is more speech, not enforced silence. Only an emergency can justify suppression. Such must be the rule if authority is to be reconciled with freedom. Such, in my opinion, is the command of the Constitution. It is, therefore, always open to Americans to challenge a law abridging free speech and assembly by showing that there was no emergency justifying it."[9]

In making that statement, Mr. Brandeis, though he keeps the traditional legal words, has abandoned the idea of "clear and present danger." He has brought us far along the road toward that very different principle of the absolute freedom of public discussion which was advocated in the first lecture of this series. Dangers, he now says, do not, as such, justify suppression. We Americans are not afraid of ideas, of any idea, if only we can have a fair chance to think about it. Under our plan of government, only an "emergency" can justify suppression.

[9] *Ibid.;* Chafee, *op. cit.,* p. 349.

And it we wish to see how far Mr. Brandeis has departed, or is departing, from the position originally taken by Mr. Holmes, we need only examine what are for him the defining characteristics of an "emergency." It is a situation in which there is "no opportunity for full discussion," in which there is no "time to expose through discussion the falsehood and fallacies, to avert the evil by the processes of education." Never when the ordinary civil processes of discussion and education are available, says Mr. Brandeis, will the Constitution tolerate the resort to suppression. The only allowable justification of it is to be found, not in the dangerous character of a specific set of ideas, but in the social situation which, for the time, renders the community incapable of the reasonable consideration of the issues of policy which confront it. In an emergency, as so defined, there can be no assurance that partisan ideas will be given by the citizens a fair and intelligent hearing. There can be no assurance that all ideas will be fairly and adequately presented. In a word, when such a civil or military emergency comes upon us, the processes of public discussion have broken down. In that situation as so defined, no advocate of the freedom of speech, however ardent, could deny the right and the duty of the government to declare that public discussion must be, not by one party alone, but by all parties alike, stopped until the order necessary for fruitful discussion has been restored. When the roof falls in, a moderator may, without violating the First Amendment, declare the meeting adjourned.

But to say these things is to deny at its very roots the principle which had been formulated by Mr. Holmes. That principle was directed toward the suppression of some one partisan set of ideas. And it did so at the same time and under the same conditions in which opposed and competing partisan ideas were allowed free expression. "Dangerous" ideas were suppressed while "safe" ideas were encouraged. The doctrine, as stated, assumed that the normal processes of free public discussion were going on. But in the very midst of those processes it attacked and punished the advocates of some one point of view on the ground that their beliefs seemed to those in authority dangerous. That procedure Mr. Brandeis, if I understand him, now flatly repudiates. "If there be time to expose through discussion the falsehood and fallacies, to avert the evil by the processes of education, the remedy to be applied is more speech, not enforced silence." The logical integrity, the social passion of Mr. Brandeis, could not tolerate the essential incoherence, the rabid intolerance, of the "clear and present danger" principle, which would give a hearing to one side while denying it to the other. His lucid and painstaking mind fought its way through the self-contradictions of that doctrine as a theory of self-government. And as he did so, he brought nearer the day when we Americans can again hold up our heads and reaffirm our loyalty to the fundamental principles of the Constitution, can say without equivocation, with confidence that the words mean what they say, "Congress shall make no law abridging the freedom of speech."

CHAPTER III

AMERICAN INDIVIDUALISM AND
THE CONSTITUTION

IN THE first and second lectures of this series we have argued that the effect of the "clear and present danger" theory of the freedom of speech, of late adopted by the Supreme Court, has been to merge the First Amendment into the Fifth. Under that interpretation, the freedom in question has become alienable rather than unalienable, subject to restriction rather than safe from restriction, a matter of circumstances rather than a matter of principle, relative rather than absolute. Public discussion has thus been reduced to the same legal status as private discussion. Individual self-seeking has been given the same constitutional rating as national provision for the general welfare. The rights of men as makers of laws are now indistinguishable from their rights as subjects of law. What men possess has the same guarantee of freedom as what they think.

Now, as already stated, the primary interest of these lectures is not in the legal problems of freedom but in the significance of those problems and their solutions for the education of American citizens in the understanding of their own political institutions. The Supreme Court, we have said, is and must be one of our most effective teachers. It is, in the last resort, an accredited interpreter to us of our own intentions. If, then, as Plato has told us, the best wisdom of men can be summed up in the phrase, "Know thyself," it is to our highest court that we must turn when we seek for wisdom concerning our relations to one another and to the government which, under the Constitution, we have established and now maintain. In this last lecture, then, we shall be trying to discover the philosophy, the view of human institutions, the theory of human destiny, out of which the "clear and present danger" principle springs. We shall be asking, also, whether or not that philosophy is valid. Does it, as I believe, cut away rather than sustain the fundamental roots of our constitutional procedure? That philosophy is, today, largely dominant over our popular thinking. It is possible, therefore, that the Supreme Court, in its recent dealings with freedom of speech, has been confirming us in our errors rather than leading us out of them. We must now try to see whether or not that suggestion is justified.

As we thus proceed with our study of the First and Fifth amendments, we must stop for a moment to take note of the interpretation which the Supreme Court has given to the Fourteenth Amendment. That interpretation throws much light upon our assertion that the two earlier provisions for the freedom of speech have now been made one.

As everyone knows, the First and Fifth amendments deal only with legislation by the federal Congress. After the Civil War, however, it was decided to lay down similar restrictions upon legislation by the several states. To this end, the Fourteenth Amendment was adopted. That amendment, therefore, in defined ways, guards the freedom of speech from "state" interference. Now, in that situation, the Supreme Court has rightly assumed that within the text of the Fourteenth Amendment, words will be found which will do in the state field what the First and Fifth together are doing in the federal field. What, then, are those words?

The clause which seems intended to carry the double burden reads as follows: "No State shall make or enforce any law which shall abridge the privileges or immunities of citizens of the United States; nor shall any State deprive any person of life, liberty, or property without due process of law; nor deny to any person within its jurisdiction the equal protection of the laws."

It is not hard, in that statement, to single out the clause which is the proper mate of the Fifth Amendment. As a matter of fact, the relevant words are directly copied from the one to the other. The statement, "nor shall any State deprive any person of life, liberty, or property without due process of law," is obviously intended to put upon state action the same restriction which the same words of the Fifth Amendment put upon federal action. In both cases, speech as a private possession, correlative with life and property, is protected from improper restrictions.

But which words of the Fourteenth Amendment reproduce, in their own field, the intention of the First Amendment? What statement corresponds to the dictum, "Congress shall make no law . . . abridging the freedom of speech"? To the nonlegal mind it would seem clear, as Mr. Brandeis once suggested, that the clause, "No State shall make or enforce any law which shall abridge the privileges or immunities of citizens of the United States," was intended to do that work. The use of the term "abridge" rather than "deprive" suggests the connection. Then, too, the freedom of speech has traditionally been regarded by us as one of our "privileges or immunities." And still again, the clause in question seems suited to match the First Amendment because it speaks, rightly or wrongly, with the same absoluteness. Its temper is not the relative mood of due process but the unqualified mood of absolute prohibition. Unfortunately, the clause in question protects "citizens" rather than "persons," and, hence, resident aliens are not provided for. And yet that difficulty is more apparent than real. The essential point is not that the alien has a right to speak but that we citizens have a right to hear him. The freedom in question is ours.

But, strange as it may seem, the Supreme Court has decided otherwise. With some hesitation and uncertainty, it has thrust aside the "privileges and immunities" clause of the Fourteenth Amendment and has chosen, in the state field, to protect both the freedom of speech of the First Amendment and that of the Fifth, under the due process clause which is taken directly from the latter. That decision clearly reveals the point of view which the court had already adopted in dealing with federal legislation. The First Amendment had been swallowed up by the Fifth. The freedom of public discussion is, therefore, no longer safe from abridgment. It is safe only from *undue* abridgment. By judicial fiat, the Constitution of the United States has been radically amended.

1

As we now seek to discover and criticize the ideas, the philosophy, which underlie the adoption of the "clear and present danger" principle, we must, of course, deal primarily with the opinions and other writings of Mr. Holmes himself. His position has, however, been given by Professor Zechariah Chafee, Jr., an explanation and elucidation which are exceedingly useful for our purpose. Mr. Chafee does not always agree with the reasonings or the conclusions of Mr. Holmes. If he follows, he does so independently. But he is, on the whole, a sympathetic interpreter. In his *Free Speech in the United States,* he develops a sustained and beautifully organized argument. And his rendering of the "clear and present danger" principle is much more explicit and systematic than that given by the inventor of the phrase. We shall be better able to understand Mr. Holmes if we first follow Mr. Chafee's argument along the two different lines which it takes.

"The First Amendment," Mr. Chafee tells us, "protects two kinds of interests in free speech. There is an individual interest, the need of many men to express their opinions on matters vital to them if life is to be worth living, and a social interest in the attainment of truth, so that the country may not only adopt the wisest course but carry it out in the wisest way."[10]

These words reveal, more sharply than anything said by Mr. Holmes, the legal meaning of the "clear and present danger"

[10] Chafee, *op. cit.,* p. 33.

thinking. Mr. Chafee separates, as we have done, the private interest in speech from the public interest in speech. But he assigns to them both the same constitutional guarantee of freedom. He places them both under the protection of the First Amendment. But the effect of that decision is identical with that which puts them both within the scope of the Fifth Amendment. There can be no doubt that a private interest in speech, as such, must be under legislative control. And "the need of many men to express their opinions" is no exception to that rule. If, then, Mr. Chafee is right, a freedom of speech protected by the First Amendment may be abridged. And from this it follows that, so far as the First Amendment is concerned, the freedom of speech in the public interest may also be abridged. By its association with private speech under a common principle, public speech is reduced to the level of "proximity and degree." The camel, once admitted to the tent, knocks it down. The right of the citizens of the United States to know what they are voting about, by an unholy union with a private desire for private satisfaction, is robbed of its virtue. The constitutional defences of public discussion have been broken through.

But as against this position taken by Mr. Chafee, it must be urged again that the absoluteness of the First Amendment rests upon the fact that it is not double-minded in reference. It is single-minded. It has no concern about the "needs of many men to express their opinions." It provides, not for many men, but for all men. The Fifth Amendment, by contrast, gives assurance that a private need to speak will get the impartial consideration to which it is entitled. But the First Amendment has other work to do. It is protecting the common needs of all the members of the body politic. It cares for the public need. And since that wider interest includes all the narrower ones insofar as they can be reconciled, it is prior to them all. The public discussion of it, therefore, has a constitutional status which no pursuit of an individual purpose can ever claim. It stands alone, as the cornerstone of the structure of self-government. If that uniqueness were taken away, government by consent of the governed would have perished from the earth.

But Mr. Chafee has a second line of argument by which the "clear and present danger" principle is clarified and defended. "The true boundary line of the First Amendment," he says, "can be fixed only when Congress and the Courts realize that the principle on which speech is classified as lawful and unlawful involves the balancing against each other of two very important social interests, in public safety and in the search for truth. Every reasonable attempt should be made to maintain both interests unimpaired and the great interest in free speech should be sacrificed only when the interest in public safety is really imperilled, and not, as most men believe, when it is barely conceivable that it may be slightly affected."[11]

That statement reveals more clearly than any other I have seen the fighting issue with respect to the Holmesian interpretation of the freedom of speech. Mr. Chafee is here puzzling, as were Mr. Holmes and Mr. Brandeis, in their earlier opinions, about action appropirate to an "emergency." But he seems to me to take the wrong road. The interest in the public safety and the interest in the search for truth are, Mr. Chafee says, two distinct interests. And they may be so balanced against each other, he says, that on occasion we must choose between them. Is that the relation between public discussion and the public welfare as it is conceived by the Constitution? I do not think so. And I can find nothing in the Constitution which justifies the assertion. Where, in that document, are we told of the balancing of which Mr. Chafee speaks? In what words is it said that if the search for truth imperils the public safety, that search shall be checked, its freedom may be abridged? There are no such words. And, more than that, the logic of the plan of self-government, as defined by the Constitution, decisively rejects the "balancing" theory which Mr. Chafee advances.

In reaching his conclusion at this point Mr. Chafee is, I am

11 *Ibid.*, p. 35.

sure, misled by his inclusion of an individual interest within the scope of the First Amendment. That private interest may, of course, be "balanced" against the public safety. The felt need of an individual to speak on a given occasion may be contrary to the common good. And, in that case, the private need, under proper safeguards, must give way. But the First Amendment, as noted in our first lecture, is not saying that any man may talk whenever and wherever he chooses. It is not dealing with that private issue. It is saying that, as interests, the integrity of public discussion and the care for the public safety are identical. We Americans, in choosing our form of government, have made, at this point, a momentous decision. We have decided to be self-governed. We have measured the dangers and the values of the suppression of the freedom of public inquiry and debate. And, on the basis of that measurement, having regard for the public safety, we have decided that the destruction of freedom is always unwise, that freedom is always expedient. The conviction recorded by that decision is not a sentimental vagary about the "natural rights" of individuals. It is a reasoned and sober judgment as to the best available method of guarding the public safety. We, the People, as we plan for the general welfare, do not choose to be "protected" from the "search for truth." On the contrary, we have adopted it as our "way of life," our method of doing the work of governing for which, as citizens, we are responsible. Shall we, then, as practitioners of freedom, listen to ideas which, being opposed to our own, might destroy confidence in our form of government? Shall we give a hearing to those who hate and despise freedom, to those who, if they had the power, would destroy our institutions? Certainly, yes! Our action must be guided, not by their principles, but by ours. We listen, not because they desire to speak, but because we need to hear. If there are arguments against our theory of government, our policies in war or in peace, we the citizens, the rulers, must hear and consider them for ourselves. That is the way of public safety. It is the program of self-government.

In his study, *Free Speech in the United States,* Mr. Chafee gives abundant evidence in support of this criticism of his position. The suppression of freedom of speech, he finds, has been throughout our history a disastrous threat to the public safety. As he sums up his results, he takes as a kind of motto the words of John Stuart Mill: "A State which dwarfs its men in order that they may be more docile instruments in its hands even for beneficial purposes, will find that with small men no great thing can really be accomplished."[12] Mr. Chafee tells the story, as he sees it, of the futility and disaster which came upon the efforts of President Wilson in World War I as he was driven, by the threat of clear and present dangers, into the suppressions of the Espionage Act.

President Wilson's tragic failure, according to Mr. Chafee, was his blindness to the imperative need of public information and public discussion bearing on the issues of war and peace. He felt bound to prevent imminent substantive evils which might arise from that discussion. In the attempt to do so, nearly two thousand persons, Mr. Chafee tells us, were prosecuted. The fruits of those prosecutions he sums up as follows: ". . . tens of thousands among those 'forward-looking men and women' to whom President Wilson had appealed in earlier years were bewildered and depressed and silenced by the negation of freedom in the twenty-year sentences requested by his legal subordinates from complacent judges. So we had plenty of patriotism and very little criticism, except of the slowness of ammunition production. Wrong courses were followed like the dispatch of troops to Archangel in 1918, which fatally alienated Russia from Wilson's aims for a peaceful Europe. Harmful facts like the secret treaties were concealed while they could have been cured, only to bob up later and wreck everything. What was equally disastrous, right positions, like our support of the League of Nations before the armistice, were taken unthinkingly merely because the President favored them; then they collapsed as soon as the excitement was over, because they had no depth and had never been hardened

12 *Ibid.,* p. 564.

by the hammer-blows of open discussion. And so, when we attained military victory, we did not know what to do with it. No well-informed public opinion existed to carry through Wilson's war aims for a new world order to render impossible the recurrence of disaster."[13]

As he writes those words, Mr. Chafee seems to me to have changed sides on his own fighting issue. He is not now judging between the interest in the search for truth and the interest in the public safety, balancing one of these against the other. That is what he accuses President Wilson of doing. On the contrary, he is shrewdly and passionately declaring that these two public interests are, in intention and in practice, identical. His complaint against President Wilson is not merely that the president curbed the search for truth. It is that, by doing so, he had made inevitable "the recurrence of disaster," had proceeded to "wreck everything." And that is the final argument upon which the absoluteness of the First Amendment rests. It does not balance intellectual freedom against public safety. On the contrary, its great declaration is that intellectual freedom is the necessary bulwark of the public safety. That declaration admits of no exceptions. If, by suppression, we attempt to avoid lesser evils, we create greater evils. We buy temporary and partial advantage at the cost of permanent and dreadful disaster. That disaster is the breakdown of self-government. Free men need the truth as they need nothing else. In the last resort, it is only the search for and the dissemination of truth that can keep our country safe.

As seen in philosophical terms, the defect in Mr. Chafee's argument becomes clear. That argument is dangerously hostile to the purposes of the Constitution because it implies a theory of the nature and function of intelligence which destroys the belief that men can govern themselves. It undermines the conviction that a man or a society can, by taking thought, guide its own actions. When men decide to be self-governed, to take control of their behavior, the search for truth is not merely one of

[13] *Ibid.*, pp. 561–562.

a number of interests which may be "balanced," on equal terms, against one another. In that enterprise, the attempt to know and to understand has a unique status, a unique authority, to which all other activities are subordinated. It tells them what to do and what not to do. It judges them. It approves and condemns their claims. It organizes them into inclusive and exclusive plans of action. It has, therefore, an authority over them all which is wholly incongruous with the notion that one of them, or all of them together, might be balanced against it. One might as well speak of the judge in a courtroom as balanced against the defendant. Political self-government comes into being only insofar as the common judgment, the available intelligence, of the community takes control over all interests, only insofar as its authority over them is recognized and is effective.

And it is that authority of these truth-seeking activities which the First Amendment recognizes as uniquely significant when it says that the freedom of public discussion shall never be abridged. It is the failure to recognize the uniqueness of that authority which has led the Supreme Court to break down the difference between the First Amendment and the Fifth. That authority is sadly misconceived or ignored when we bring under the same constitutional protection both our possessions and our wisdom in the use of those possessions. Under the Bill of Rights it is "we" who "govern" our possessions. It is "we" and not "they" that must be free. If we break down that basic distinction we have lost sight of the responsibilities and the dignity of a "citizen." We have failed to see the role which public intelligence plays in the life of a democracy. We have made impossible the understanding and the teaching of government by consent of the governed.

2

Our argument now turns to Mr. Holmes himself, the leading hero, or villain, of the plot. And, first of all, we must pay tribute to his leadership in the defense of the freedom of speech for half a century. He was a gay and gallant gentleman. No man of his time so captured and excited the spirit of young fighters for Civil Liberties as did he. More effectively than any of his associates he called upon his fellow citizens, young and old, to criticize their prejudices, to dig deep in search for the meaning of their political institutions. The Magnificent Yankee was one of the very great teachers of political freedom.

And yet the thinking of Mr. Holmes about the First Amendment has no such excellence. Without giving the slightest justification in fact or in principle, he thrust into the interpretation of that formula the blank assertion that certain kinds of speech "will not be endured." He declared that if "clear and present danger" is involved, the suppression of speech may be, on that ground, justified. Those assertions were not supported by constitutional reasons. What then, is, for him, the source of these beliefs?

As we seek acquaintance with the mind of Mr. Holmes, we must remember that he brought to the interpretation of the Constitution the results of an eager and lifelong preoccupation with the problems of philosophy. He loved to read, to reflect, to debate with his friends, about men and the universe. His exploring mind searched for those deeper springs of belief and preference and action from which have come the rushing currents of the Constitution. He studied thinking and its uses in the struggle for political freedom. And his opinions on constitutional questions give record of the conclusions which he reached by means of those studies. We cannot, therefore, validly accept or reject his interpretations of our legal customs, unless we meet him on this, his own, ground. We, too, must philosophize. With him we must go down as deep as we can to examine the moral and intellectual foundations of a self-governing society.

The philosophy of Mr. Holmes was, we shall find, one of excessive individualism. In it there is to be found a strange mingling of the new Darwinism of his day, which had not yet found its meaning, with an old and outworn Puritanism which had lost its ancient virtue. And to these two factors, the early experiences of Mr. Holmes in the Civil War had added the martial spirit of the reminiscent and even sentimental soldier. With these divisive influences at the back of his mind, Mr. Holmes sees a human society as a multitude of individuals, each struggling for his own existence, each living his own life, each saving his own soul, if he has a soul to save, in the social forms of a competitive independence. Always, therefore, he tends to interpret the constitutional cooperation of one hundred and more millions of Americans, together with the past and future generations who belong to the same community, as if they had no fundamental community of purpose at all. The theory of strife he can understand—but not the theory of cooperation. A nation tends to be, for his mind, a huge collocation of externally related human atoms.

It is largely because of the effectiveness of his expression of this individualism that Mr. Holmes stands out as one of the most representative men of his time and country. He differs from his fellow Americans, not in his beliefs, but in the clarity and fearlessness with which he expresses those beliefs. His mind is too honest to evade an issue, too incisive to overlook it. He has an unusual power for devising sharp and challenging phrases. He can say to us what we ourselves would say if we were not too busy to examine our own ideas, too prudent and worldly-wise to risk the danger of discovering what those ideas mean. For these reasons he has, at the present crisis in our history, a peculiar significance for his fellow countrymen. In him we can see ourselves, as it were, under high illumination. And if, as seems obvious, the time has come when leadership in the world has brought to us responsibility for understanding what men are, and where they are going, and why, there can be no doubt that the opinions of Mr. Holmes about self-government provide materials for study on which the mind of every loyal American should be busily at work. That assertion is even more true when we assume Mr.

Holmes to be wrong than it is when and where we assume him to be right.

As a student of philosophy, Mr. Holmes was, of course, deeply interested in the relation between the machinery of the law and the moral purpose of justice. His reflections upon that relation, though partial, were keen and incisive. With the zest of a good craftsman, he was, in legal theory, a mechanist. The activities of legislatures and courts he sees, from this point of view, simply as a play of forces which are in conflict. And he delights in the technical game of the manipulation of those forces. He follows the ups and downs of the contests of the law with lively interest and, at times, it must be said, with ironical glee. Human living is, he tells us, "a roar of bargain and battle." And though, as a dispassionate spectator, he is convinced that there is little, if anything, to be gained by the fighting except the fun of the fighting itself, Mr. Holmes, as a good soldier, plunges gloriously into the conflict.

That Mr. Holmes is a mechanist in legal theory is shown by his fascinating description of "The Path of the Law," in a speech given at the Boston University School of Law in 1897. "If you want to know the law and nothing else," he said, "you must look at it as a bad man, who cares only for the material consequences which such knowledge enables him to predict, not as a good one, who finds his reasons for conduct, whether inside the law or outside of it, in the vaguer sanctions of conscience."[14] And again, "But, as I shall try to show, a legal duty so-called is nothing but a prediction that if a man does or omits certain things he will be made to suffer in this way or that by judgment of the court—and so of a legal right."[15] And still again, "People want to know under what circumstances and how far they will run the risk of coming against what is so much stronger than themselves, and hence it becomes a business to find out when this danger is to be

[14] Oliver Wendell Holmes, *Collected Legal Papers*. New York, Harcourt, Brace and Howe, 1920, p. 17.
[15] *Ibid.*, p. 169.

feared. The object of our study, then, is prediction, the prediction of the incidence of the public force through the instrumentality of the courts."[16]

With the exception of the phrase, "the vaguer sanctions of conscience," these statements are impressive, both in their audacity and in their validity. As a technician, Mr. Holmes strips "the business of the law" of all "moral" implications. Legal battles he finds to be fought in terms of the conflict of interests, individual and social. Their results are the victories and defeats of forces and counterforces. And they are, for the technician, nothing else, except, it may be, a source of revenue. This is magnificent, clearheaded legal technology.

But there is a philosophic weakness in this mechanistic theory which can be stated in two different ways. First, being partial, it gives no adequate account of the deeper social ends and ideas upon which the legal procedure depends for life and meaning. These battles of which Mr. Holmes speaks are not fought in a jungle, in a moral vacuum. They are fought in the legislatures and courts which have been established by a self-governing society. They are not mere conflicts of interest. They are conflicts under laws which define a public interest. They are, therefore, fought by agreement as well as by difference—an agreement which is accepted by both sides. That agreement provides judges and juries whose duty it is to determine not merely what is going to happen, but what, under our plan of life, should happen. The fighting goes on under a Constitution in which We, the People, have formulated and made authoritative our deepest convictions concerning the welfare of men and of society. And Mr. Holmes' description of the legal machinery, valid as it is technologically, provided these deeper and wider meanings be given assured control, is utterly invalid if it be taken as an account of the total legal process. On this basis it seems fair to say that, as he interprets the freedom of speech which the Constitution protects, the one thing to which Mr. Holmes, the mech-

[16] *Ibid.*, p. 167.

anist, does not pay attention is the Constitution itself. One finds in his arguing little reference to the fact that we of the United States have decided to be a self-governing community. There is not much said about a fundamental agreement among us to which we have pledged "our Lives, our Fortunes, and our sacred Honor." We are, for the argument, merely a horde of fighting individuals, restrained or supported by laws which "happen" to be on the books.

The same conclusion will be reached if we examine carefully what Mr. Holmes says about "the vaguer sanctions of conscience," the demands and principles of morality. As we read his words about law and morality we must recognize that it is not strictly accurate to say that he takes no account whatever of the moral factor. It would be more true to say that he is troubled by it, that he does not know where to place it. As he studies legislation and litigation, morality constantly thrusts itself forward as a disturbing influence which threatens to clog the legal machinery. Mr. Holmes has told us that one cannot understand the law unless one looks at it as a bad man. But meanwhile, he is aware that men are, in some respects, good, even when they are dealing with the law. In the very midst of the conflicting forces of interest Mr. Holmes finds "other things" such as "a good man's reasons for conduct," revealing themselves and claiming relevance. In his statement of the mechanistic theory he says, ". . . I ask you for the moment to imagine yourselves indifferent to other and greater things."[17] But the account of these other things when Mr. Holmes, in other moments, comes back to them, is vague, unclear, and shifting. As contrasted with the sharp and skillful phrases which describe the battles of the courts, the descriptions of morality are neither sharp nor skillful. The mind of Mr. Holmes deals easily, and even merrily, with the "bad man." But the "good man," as an object of philosophical inquiry, mystifies and confuses him. The bad man is clear—too clear to be true. He wants to know what he can get away with.

[17] *Ibid.*, p. 170.

He wants a prediction of the differing consequences of law-breaking, and of law-observance, so that he may have a ground for choosing between them. He hires a lawyer to tell him. The lawyer does what he is paid to do. And Mr. Holmes delights in beating them both at their own game. But meanwhile, what of the good man? What does he want? What is he trying to find out when, if ever, he goes to his lawyer? To those questions Mr. Holmes has no ready answer. His thought has very great difficulty in piercing through the legal machinery to discover those elements of human fellowship and virtue for the sake of which good men have established and maintained, against the assaults of bad men and their legal advisers, the laws and the Constitution of the United States. As against the dogma of Mr. Holmes I would venture to assert the counterdogma that one cannot understand the basic purposes of our Constitution as a judge or a citizen should understand them, unless one sees them as a good man, a man who, in his political activities, is not merely fighting for what, under the law, he can get, but is eagerly and generously serving the common welfare.

3

With respect to the nature of goodness, Mr. Holmes has two very different and conflicting sets of opinions. And it is his failure to resolve that conflict which seems to me to lie at the root of his misinterpretation of the First Amendment. We must, therefore, examine more carefully what he has to say about the principles of right behavior.

On the one hand, scattered through his meditations are such statements as the following:

For my own part, I believe that the struggle for life is the order of the world, at which it is vain to repine.[18]

With all humility I think, "Whatever thy hand finds to do, do

[18] Oliver Wendell Holmes, *Speeches*. Boston, Little, Brown & Co., 1934, p. 58.

it with thy might," infinitely more important than the vain attempt to love one's neighbor as one's self.[19]

But, in the last resort, a man rightly prefers his own interest to that of his neighbors. And this is as true of legislation as in any other form of corporate action.[20]

The fact is that legislation in this country, as well as elsewhere . . . is necessarily made a means by which a body, having the power, puts burdens which are disagreeable to them on the shoulders of some one else.[21]

But it seems to me clear that the ultima ratio, not only regum, but of private persons, is force, and that at the bottom of all private relations, however tempered by sympathy, and all the social feelings, is a justifiable self-preference.[22]

Self-preference and force—those are the basic principles of human behavior. According to those principles, a good man takes what he can get. If there are burdens to bear, he sees to it that someone else bears them. Such self-interest should, of course, be intelligent, that is, shrewd. But it is, nonetheless, interest in self. It is not interest in the welfare of others.

But Mr. Holmes cannot be content to leave the matter there. He has another theory of goodness. His phrase, "the vaguer sanctions of conscience," indicates his awareness that, in the midst of all the force and self-preference, another human factor is at work. Of that factor he can speak with an adoring rapture. But his words about it have no clarity. They express little more than mystical meaninglessness. "Life," he tells us, "is a roar of bargain and battle, but in the very heart of it, there rises a mystic spiritual tone that gives meaning to the whole. It transmutes the dull detail into romance. It reminds us that our only but adequate significance is as parts of the unimaginable whole. It suggests

[19] Ibid., p. 85.
[20] Max Lerner, The Mind and Faith of Justice Holmes. Boston, Little, Brown & Co., 1943, p. 50.
[21] Ibid., p. 51.
[22] Ibid., p. 59.

that while we think we are egotists, we are living to ends outside ourselves."[23]

Are we living to ends outside ourselves? If so, neither Mr.
Holmes nor we can rightly think that we are altogether egotists.
That "suggestion," as he calls it, is either valid or invalid. And
if it is valid, the entire structure of explanation in terms of force
and self-preference becomes untenable. It must be abandoned.
If the universe as a whole is unimaginable then neither a mystic
spiritual tone nor anything else has given meaning to it. It has
no meaning. Why pretend that it has? If the dull detail of life
is merely selfishness, one can be romantic about it only by sheer
self-deception. The words which Mr. Holmes here writes are
thrilling in their rhetorical beauty, but they are disastrous in their
effect upon the human understanding of human goodness. And
his failure at this point is crucial for our argument because, whatever else it may mean, the First Amendment is an expression of
human goodness. That amendment, in its own field, stands guard
over the general welfare of the community. It protects men as
they engage in the moral endeavor to advance that welfare. If
that endeavor be reduced to meaninglessness it is little wonder
that, in the same hands, the First Amendment has suffered the
same fate.

This failure of Mr. Holmes to recognize the sane and solid
moral principles which find expression in our national agreement
that government shall be carried on only by consent of the governed is obvious at every turn of his writing. His romantic
morality has no chance whatever when it comes into conflict
with his clear-eyed, tough-minded technology. The outcome of
such a battle is readily seen in the well-known letter to Mr. Wu,
in which he enters vigorous and radical objection to the moral
idealism which says that, under our form of government, every
citizen has, and has a right to have, dignity—the dignity of men
who govern themselves. With scorn for such idealism, Mr. Holmes
writes, "I don't believe that it is an absolute principle or even a

[23] Holmes, *Speeches*, p. 97.

human ultimate that man is always an end in himself—that his dignity must be respected, etc. We march up a conscript with bayonets behind to die for a cause he doesn't believe in. And I feel no scruples about it. Our morality seems to me only a check on the ultimate domination of force, just as our politeness is a check on the impulse of every pig to put his feet in the trough."[24]

One pig against another! Or, perhaps better, a lot of pigs against one! What shall we say of the man who thus explains the courtesies and the moralities of human society? Harold Laski has just closed a glowing tribute to his revered master with the words, "I have known no man who lived on the heights in whom nobility and kindness were at once so effortless and so spacious in their dignified serenity."[25] And many of us who knew him, closely or not so closely, in and around his home on Eye Street in Washington, were deeply moved by the same affection and admiration. But to say that is to speak of the personal quality of Mr. Holmes, rather than of his ideas. And it was a set of ideas, a theory of morality, which ran deeply through all his reflections and seeped down into his interpretations of the Constitution. It is that set of ideas, that theory of morality, which we must critically judge if we seek to determine the validity of the opinions which Mr. Holmes wrote.

Many of us, I am sure, agree with him that the dignity of man is not an absolute principle, if by that is meant a principle of the universe. So far as we can see, the non-human universe has no moral principles. It neither knows nor cares about human dignity, nor about anything else. And further, we may agree that respect for human dignity is not a *human* ultimate. That attitude of mutual regard is created and justified only insofar as groups of men have succeeded in binding themselves together into a fellowship which, by explicit or implicit compact, maintains a "way of life." And that goal is, for humanity as a whole, still far

[24] Lerner, *op. cit.*, p. 431.
[25] Harold Laski, "Ever Sincerely Yours, O. W. Holmes," book review in the *New York Times Magazine*, February 15, 1948.

off. But when, in the face of our Constitution, someone says that a *fellow citizen* has no "dignity" which "must be respected"— that is another matter. To say that is not merely to ignore the Constitution. It is to deny it. Mr. Holmes, in those words, flatly repudiates the moral compact on which our plan of self-government rests. And, especially, he breaks down the basic principle of the First Amendment. As one makes this accusation, one must, of course, recognize the difference between the intention of our institutions and their success in realizing that intention. Everyone knows how partial is our achievement in the maintaining of self-government. In large measure, we live and act without dignity. But the essential point is that we are pledged together to create a society in which men shall have the status of governors of themselves. They must move, not with bayonets behind, but with purposes ahead. And if we fail in that, as we do, we must have "scruples about it." If we submit to our failure without regret, without scruple, we have abandoned the Constitution. We have divided our community into the "we" who have dignity and the "they" who have not. The battle of the Constitution has been lost.

4

Now, with these reflections of Mr. Holmes in mind, we are ready, or should be ready, to take the final step in our argument. We must now read and try to interpret the famous dissenting opinion in the Abrams case, in which Mr. Holmes explicitly stated the positive theory of the Constitution insofar as it relates to the principle of the freedom of speech. The opinion reads, in part, as follows:

Persecution for the expression of opinions seems to me perfectly logical. If you have no doubt of your premises or power and want a certain result with all your heart you naturally express your wishes in law and sweep away all opposition. To allow opposition by speech seems to indicate that you think the speech impotent, as when a man says that he has squared the circle, or that you do not care wholeheartedly for the result, or that you doubt either your power or your premises. But when men have realized that time has upset many fighting faiths, they may come to believe even more than they believe the very foundations of their own conduct that the ultimate good desired is better reached by free trade in ideas—that the best test of truth is the power of the thought to get itself accepted in the competition of the market; and that truth is the only ground upon which their wishes safely can be carried out. That at any rate is the theory of our Constitution. It is an experiment, as all life is an experiment. Every year if not every day we have to wager our salvation upon some prophecy based on imperfect knowledge. While that experiment is part of our system I think we should be eternally vigilant against attempts to check the expression of opinions that we loathe and believe to be fraught with death, unless they so imminently threaten immediate interference with the lawful and pressing purposes of the law that an immediate check is required to save the country. I wholly disagree with the argument of the government that the First Amendment left the common law as to seditious libel in force. History seems to me against the notion. I had conceived that the United States through many years had shown its repentance for the Sedition Act of July 14, 1798, by repaying fines that it imposed. Only the emergency that makes it immediately dangerous to leave the correction of evil counsels to time warrants making any exception to the sweeping command, "Congress shall make no law . . . abridging the freedom of speech."[26]

These words are beautifully written. They are at once provocative and deeply moving. Mr. Justice Frankfurter has said of them, "It is not reckless prophecy to assume that his famous dissenting opinion in the Abrams case will live so long as English prose retains its power to move."[27] And Max Lerner, speaking with like hot admiration, has told us, "I can add little to what has been said of Holmes' language. It has economy, grace, final-

[26] 250 U.S. 616. Chafee, *op. cit.*, pp. 136–137.
[27] Felix Frankfurter, *Justice Holmes and The Supreme Court.* Cambridge, Mass., Harvard University Press, 1938, pp. 54–55.

ity, and it is the greatest utterance on intellectual freedom by an American, ranking in the English language with Milton and Mill."[28]

An American teacher, reading those words, may join heartily in praise of the rhetorical excellence of the opinion. But its meaning, its logic, have no such excellence. In form it is, as Mr. Lerner says, one of our greatest utterances. But in content Mr. Holmes, here as elsewhere, has spoken eloquently for an American Individualism whose excesses have weakened and riddled our understanding of the meaning of intellectual freedom. To that negative criticism, however, two exceptions must be made.

First, no one who is sensitive to the human values at stake in the case under consideration can fail to thrill with admiration of the gallant conclusion in which Mr. Holmes condemns the judgment of his colleagues. In the lower court, after one of the most disgraceful trials ever held in the history of the nation, a group of helpless, ineffectual Russian immigrants had been literally thrown to the wild beasts of prejudice and hatred which war had let loose upon the country. And their crime was that they had advocated policies which, at the same time, were being urged upon President Wilson by some of his wisest advisers. Those advisers were not indicted and convicted and punished, even though their words might have been expected to have far greater effect. But the defenseless rebels were sentenced to jail for periods ranging up to twenty years. For his castigation of that shameful legal crime, Mr. Holmes will be remembered and honored so long as the Constitution endures.

And, further, we must accept and applaud the assertion that the Constitution is an experiment, in the sense in which all life is an experiment. Our plan of government, being based on imperfect knowledge, must be forever open to amendment, forever on trial. It will change as social conditions change, and as human insight changes. And no one can tell in advance how slow or

[28] Lerner, *op. cit.,* p. 306.

how quick, how superficial or how radical, those changes will be. We, the People, acting under the Constitution, will decide, from time to time, on that issue. And our successors will be free, as we are, to determine what form, for them, the government shall take.

But the remarks of Mr. Holmes upon the central issue of the case before him—upon the testing of truth and upon the using of truth in the service of the common welfare—have no such adequacy. He does not, I am sure, at either of these points, give us, as he intends to do, "the theory of our Constitution."

First, there is undeniably a genuine, though partial, validity in the dictum that "the best test of truth is the power of the thought to get itself accepted in the competition of the market." It rightly tells us that the only truth which we self-governing men can rely on is that which we win for ourselves in the give and take of public discussion and decision. What we together think at any time is, for us, our truth at that time. And, in the sense in which words are here used, that test of truth is not merely the "best" test. There is no other. But that partial insight has often been interpreted, by the individualism which Mr. Holmes represents, to be a total characterization of the truth-seeking process. And, in that form, it has become, in our American public life, a fruitful source of intellectual irresponsibility and of the errors which irresponsibility brings. We Americans, when thinking in that vein, have taken the "competition of the market" principle to mean that as separate thinkers, we have no obligation to test our thinking, to make sure that it is worthy of a citizen who is one of "the rulers of the nation." That testing is to be done, we believe, not by us, but by "the competition of the market." Each one of us, therefore, feels free to think as he pleases, to believe whatever will serve his own private interests. We think, not as members of the body politic of "We, the People of the United States," but as farmers, as trade-union workers, as employers, as investors. We plan and vote for cotton or beets or silver or steel or wheat. Our ideas belong to the East or the West or the North or the South or the Middle. And our aim, as we debate in those capacities, is not that of finding the truth. The competition of the market will take care of that. Our aim is to "make a case," to win a fight, to make our plea plausible, to keep the pressure on. And the intellectual degradation which that interpretation of truth-testing has brought upon the minds of our people is almost unbelievable. Under its influence, there are no standards for determining the difference between the true and the false. The truth is what a man or an interest or a nation can get away with. That dependence upon intellectual laissez-faire, more than any other single factor, has destroyed the foundations of our national education, has robbed of their meaning such terms as "reasonableness" and "intelligence," and "devotion to the general welfare." It has made intellectual freedom indistinguishable from intellectual license. And to that disastrous end the beautiful words of Mr. Holmes have greatly contributed.

But the other argument of Mr. Holmes, which deals with the using of truth as well as its testing, bears more directly upon our constitutional question. It may be summarized in two statements. First, says Mr. Holmes, men are naturally intolerant. And they are rightly so. Suppression of the hostile opinions of others is justified. It is justified on grounds of self-preference, backed by force. But, second, men have learned by experience that intolerance does not pay. We need the truth as a basis for our actions. But the truth is better attained if men trade ideas freely than it is if each man stays within the limits of his own discoveries. A man's ideas must, therefore, be subjected to the competition of the market. His own self-interest requires of him that his right and natural disposition toward suppression must give way before the clear necessity of trading ideas with anyone else who is studying the same problems.

Is that the theory because of which the Constitution forbids the abridging of the freedom of speech? It is a part of it, but only, I am sure, a secondary and individualistic part. No one can deny that the winning of the truth is important for the purposes of self-government. But that is not our deepest need. Far more essential, if men are to be their own rulers, is the demand that whatever truth may become available shall be placed at the disposal of all the citizens of the community. The First Amendment is not, primarily, a device for the winning of new truth, though that is very important. It is a device for the sharing of whatever truth has been won. Its purpose is to give to every voting member of the body politic the fullest possible participation in the understanding of those problems with which the citizens of a self-governing society must deal. When a free man is voting, it is not enough that the truth is known by someone else, by some scholar or administrator or legislator. The voters must have it, all of them. The primary purpose of the First Amendment is, then, that all the citizens shall, so far as possible, understand the issues which bear upon our common life. That is why no idea, no opinion, no doubt, no belief, no counterbelief, no relevant information, may be kept from them. Under the compact upon which the Constitution rests, it is agreed that men shall not be governed by others, that they shall govern themselves. But the competitive individualism of Mr. Holmes, when it gets hold of him, drives out of his mind the existence of that compact. As he thus reads the First Amendment, his interest is directed, not toward the public freedom which is required for the purposes of self-government, but toward the private freedom of this or that individual who is seeking to understand. And for that reason, he robs the amendment of its essential meaning—the meaning of our common agreement that, working together as a body politic, we will be our own rulers. That meaning is the highest insight which men have reached in their search for political freedom. And Mr. Holmes—at least in his "clear and present danger" thinking—misses it.

5

Here, then, are the charges which I would bring against the "clear and present danger" theory. They are all, it is clear, differing forms of the basic accusation that the compact of self-government has been ignored or repudiated.

First, the theory denies or obscures the fact that free citizens have two distinct sets of civil liberties. As the makers of the laws, they have duties and responsibilities which require an absolute freedom. As the subjects of the laws, they have possessions and rights, to which belongs a relative freedom.

Second, the theory fails to keep clear the distinction between the constitutional status of discussions of public policy and the corresponding status of discussions of private policy.

Third, the theory fails to recognize that, under the Constitution, the freedom of advocacy or incitement to action *by the government* may never be abridged. It is only advocacy or incitement to action by individuals or nonpolitical groups which is open to regulation.

Fourth, the theory regards the freedom of speech as a mere device which is to be abandoned when dangers threaten the public welfare. On the contrary, it is the very presence of those dangers which makes it imperative that, in the midst of our fears, we remember and observe a principle upon whose integrity rests the entire structure of government by consent of the governed.

Fifth, the Supreme Court, by adopting a theory which annuls the First Amendment, has struck a disastrous blow at our national education. It has denied the belief that men can, by processes of free public discussion, govern themselves.

6

"Congress shall make no law . . . abridging the freedom of speech . . ."

That principle of the Constitution tells us that we may attack the Constitution in public discussion as freely as we may defend it. It gives us freedom to believe in and to advocate socialism or communism, just as some of our fellow citizens are advocating capitalism. It declares that the suppressive activities of the Federal Bureau of Invesigation, of the un-American Activities Committees, of the Department of Justice and its Immigration Service, of the President's Loyalty Order—all these are false in theory and therefore disastrous in practice. It tells us that such books as Hitler's *Mein Kampf*, or Lenin's *The State and the Revolution*, or the *Communist Manifesto* of Engels and Marx, may be freely printed, freely sold, freely distributed, freely read, freely discussed, freely believed, freely disbelieved, throughout the United States. And the purpose of that provision is not to protect the need of Hitler or Lenin or Engels or Marx "to express his opinions on matters vital to him if life is to be worth living." We are not defending the financial interests of a publisher, or a distributor, or even of a writer. We are saying that the citizens of the United States will be fit to govern themselves under their own institutions only if they have faced squarely and fearlessly everything that can be said in favor of those institutions, everything that can be said against them.

The unabridged freedom of public discussion is the rock on which our government stands. With that foundation beneath us, we shall not flinch in the face of any clear and present—or, even, terrific—danger.

CHAPTER IV

REFLECTIONS

NO ARGUMENT about principles is, I suppose, ever finished. But the argument of these lectures seems to the writer of them, peculiarly incomplete. They constitute, it seems to me, not an inquiry, but only the beginning of an inquiry. Even if it be agreed that the "clear and present danger" formula denies rather than expresses the meaning of the Constitution, even if we are convinced that the guarantee of the freedom of public discussion which is provided by the First Amendment admits of no exceptions, we are, because of those very conclusions, plunged at once into a multitude of bewildering questions. Those questions relate both to theory and to practice. And this book makes no pretense of having specifically dealt with them. In these closing reflections, the attempt will be made to indicate some lines along which further study of the meaning of the freedom of speech might go.

1

There is immediate and urgent need that We, the People of the United States, should win clarity of mind on that mutual agreement of ours concerning speech, which is recorded in the First Amendment. These lectures have tried to show that the "clear and present danger" formula, as dealt with in the discussions of the Supreme Court, has not been able to keep either its original meaning or its validity. In the keen, shrewd competition of that market place, its verbal victory has become equivocal and empty. But in the wider market of popular discussion, the dominance of the seductive phrase, in its original meaning, is clear and unmistakable. Our people are, in general, convinced that, by authority of the Supreme Court, whenever or wherever the "American Way of Life," so-called, is criticized, is declared inferior to some other set of beliefs and institutions, we are, under the Constitution, justified in resorting to the suppression of civil liberties, including the freedom of speech. This disloyalty of ours to our own plan of government, with all its dreadful consequences, now threatens to run riot through every phase of American life, including that of government. And, for that threat of disaster, the Supreme Court, on the ground of its acceptance of the phrase, must be held largely responsible. May a teacher venture to suggest that the time has come when the court, as teacher, must declare, in unequivocal terms, that no idea may be suppressed because someone in office, or out of office, has judged it to be "dangerous"?

2

If, however, as our argument has tried to show, the principle of the freedom of speech is derived, not from some supposed "Natural Right," but from the necessities of self-government by universal suffrage, there follows at once a very large limitation of the scope of the principle. The guarantee given by the First Amendment is not, then, assured to all speaking. It is assured only to speech which bears, directly or indirectly, upon issues with which voters have to deal—only, therefore, to the consideration of matters of public interest. Private speech, or private interest in speech, on the other hand, has no claim whatever to the protection of the First Amendment. If men are engaged, as we so commonly are, in argument, or inquiry, or advocacy, or incitement which is directed toward our private interests, private privileges, private possessions, we are, of course, entitled to "due process" protection of those activities. But the First Amendment

has no concern over such protection. That pronouncement remains forever confused and unintelligible unless we draw sharply
and clearly the line which separates the public welfare of the
community from the private goods of any individual citizen or
group of citizens.

What, then, is the distinction between, and the relation between, the common good and our many different private goods?
On no problem of our national life is the American mind more
confused than on this problem. And nowhere else is the need for
clarity and sanity more imperative.

Every one of us, of course, recognizes, in words, the distinction
between public and private welfare. We know, clearly or vaguely,
that under the American plan of self-government every citizen
has two radically different sets of purposes and hence two radically different relations to the governing authority, which he and
his fellows maintain. If men are free, they have two sets of values.
They "care for" their country. But they care, also, for themselves.
On the one hand, each of us, as a citizen, has a part to play in
the governing of the nation. In that capacity, we think and speak
and plan and act for the general good. On the other hand, each
of us, as an individual or as a member of some private group,
is rightly pursuing his own advantage, is seeking his own welfare.
In the first of these roles, we are voters, lawmakers, rulers. Taken
together in that role, We, the People, are the government. But,
in the second role, we are, as individuals, governed. Our constitutional agreement is that each man's individual possessions
and activities shall be subject to regulation by laws which he is
bound to obey. His private rights, including the right of "private"
speech, are liable to such abridgments as the general welfare may
require.

Here, then, are our two sets of human interests and activities,
which, under the Constitution, are given, and must be given,
fundamentally different status. How are they related? What is
the bearing of the common good on my goods—and upon yours?
Are they identical? Are they different, but congruous? Are they

opposed? Are they mutually indifferent to one another? Unless this relation can be made clear, nothing which has to do with political freedom can be understood.

We cannot, of course, in a few words analyze adequately all the implications of the Constitution with respect to public and private goods. Nor, it must be said, could we do so if many words were available. The human relations involved in the distinction between the general welfare and individual advantage are deeply and permanently perplexing. We can mention here only a few phases of the relationship which touch upon the problem of the freedom of speech.

In the Preamble to the Constitution there are listed in summary fashion the items of public interest which the body politic of the United States has adopted as its own. These are: A more perfect union, justice, domestic tranquillity, the common defense, the general welfare, the blessings of liberty. These ends or purposes We, the People, hold in common. For these we plan and work together. They are the objects of our common loyalty. How, then, do they bear upon our distinctive desires and activities as separate individuals? In answer to this question, five observations may be made.

First, in our American society, as we intend it to be, the public interest is not another different interest superimposed upon our individual desires and intentions. It is compounded out of them. It includes nothing which is not included by them. The common purpose is made up out of the separate purposes of the citizens. So far as possible, it combines them all.

But, second, since human interests are in constant conflict with one another, they cannot all be realized. We cannot make the common good by simply adding them together. To give play to one of them means often to deny play to others. And, for this reason, the public interest cannot be merely the totality of the private interests. It is, of necessity, an organization of them, a selection and arrangement, based upon judgment of relative values and mutual implications.

Third, the judgments which a government makes between interests are based upon such general principles as unity, justice, tranquillity, defense, welfare, equality, liberty. For the sake of these common demands as expressed in impartial laws, any given individual in any given situation may be required to suffer the loss of his life, his liberty, his property, his happiness. And the government which guards the common welfare is authorized, by due process, to make and, if need be, to enforce the decision that those sacrifices are needful. Some millions of the young men and women of our nation and of other nations have recently learned, and are still learning, by actual experience what that statement means.

Fourth, the activities of the government as it cares for the public interest and, thereby, for the private interests which constitute it, are both negative and positive. On the one hand, the government protects individuals and groups by enforcing prohibitions against arson, monopoly, murder, and the like. On the other hand, by supplying such facilities as roads, postal service, parks, pensions, collective bargaining, soil conservation, libraries, schools, colleges, and a host of other forms of social wealth, We, the People, carry on constructive enterprises which individuals, as such, cannot so well carry on for themselves and for their fellows.

And, fifth, it should be noted that the Constitution does not, in principle, prescribe what share of the activities needed for furthering the common good shall be directly exercised by the government and what share shall be reserved to individuals, acting separately. At this point, there is sharp division of opinion among us. There are members of our body politic who tell us that the public interest is best served when government action is reduced to a minimum and especially when it is kept negative in character. But just now, the nation as a whole seems to be moving rather swiftly and decisively—as is the world as a whole —in the opposite direction. More and more, we Americans are initiating new forms of positive government action for the common good. Between these two tendencies the struggle becomes every day more open and more intense. And as we wage that conflict it is well to remember that the logic of the Constitution gives no backing to either of the two combatants, as against the other. We are left free, as any self-governing people must leave itself free, to determine by specific decisions what our economy shall be. It would be ludicrous to say that we are committed by the Constitution to the economic cooperations of socialism. But equally ludicrous are those appeals by which, in current debate, we are called upon to defend the practices of capitalism, of "free enterprise," so-called, as essential to the freedom of the American Way of Life. The American Way of Life is free because it is what we Americans freely choose—from time to time—that it shall be.

3

The statement that the First Amendment stands guard over the freedom of public speech but is indifferent to the rights of private speech has sharp and, at times, decisive implications for many issues of civil liberty now in dispute among us. It would be a fascinating and important task to follow those implications as they bear upon the rights to freedom which are claimed, for example, by lobbyists for special interests, by advertisers in press or radio, by picketing labor unions, by Jehovah's Witnesses, by the distributors of handbills on city streets, by preachers of racial intolerance, and many others. In all these cases the crucial task is that of separating public and private claims. But such discussion would go far beyond the limits of the present inquiry. I must, however, mention one new issue which is startling, and even shocking in its threat to what has been traditionally regarded as one of our primary "public" freedoms. We have assumed that the studies of the "scholar" must have, in all respects, the absolute protection of the First Amendment. But with the devising of "atomic" and "bacteriological" knowledge for the use of, and under the direction of, military forces, we can now see how loose and inaccurate, at this point, our thinking has been. Under present circumstances it is criminally stupid to describe the inquiries of scholarship as merely "the disinterested pursuit of knowledge for its own sake." Both public and private interests are clearly involved. They subsidize much of our scholarship. And the clashes among them may bring irretrievable disaster to mankind. It may be, therefore, that the time has come when the guarding of human welfare requires that we shall abridge the private desire of the scholar—or of those who subsidize him —to study whatever he may please. It may be that the freedom of the "pursuit of truth" must, in that sense, be abridged. And, if such action were taken with that motivation, the guarantee of the First Amendment would not, in my opinion, have been violated. As I write these words, I am not taking a final stand on the issue which is here suggested. But I am sure that the issue is coming upon us and cannot be evaded. In a rapidly changing world, another of our ancient sanctities—the holiness of research —has been brought under question.

4

If the meaning and validity of the First Amendment be derived from the principles of self-government, still another very serious limitation of its scope must be recognized. The principle of the unqualified freedom of public speech is, then, valid only in and for a society which is self-governing. It has no political justification where men are governed without their consent. For example, in such social institutions as an army or a prison or an insane asylum, the principle of freedom of speech is neither relevant nor valid. Those communities are not governed by the consent of their members. That statement should, perhaps, be mitigated in the case of an army whose soldiers are also citizens of a free body politic to which the commanders of the army are responsible. And, in lesser degree, the same limitation holds true for the management of an asylum or a prison. And yet, in all these cases, the immediate fact of control without consent remains. Policies and actions are not decided on the basis of general discussion and voting by the group. There is, therefore, no political ground for the demand that discussion within the institution shall be free from abridgment.

The same irrelevance is evident when we examine the military control of a nation which has been conquered in war. On December 16, 1944, General Eisenhower issued a proclamation prescribing plans for education in Germany during military occupation. One section of his order reads as follows: "German teachers will be instructed to eliminate from their teaching anything which: (A) Glorifies militarism, expounds the practice of war or of mobilization and preparation for war, whether in the scientific, economic, or industrial fields, or the study of military geography; (B) Seeks to propagate, revive, or justify the doctrines of Nazism or to extol the achievements of Nazi leaders; (C) Favors a policy of discrimination on grounds of race or religion; (D) Is hostile to or seeks to disturb the relations between any of the United Nations. Any infringement of these provisions will be cause for immediate dismissal and punishment."

In those words, which would be utterly intolerable if applied to the teachers of the United States, the official representative of the nations which had fought for freedom, denies freedom of speech to the German teachers. And that decision, whether wise or unwise, cannot be challenged on the ground that it violates the freedom of teaching. During the period of military occupation, Germany is not self-governing. She, and her teachers, must therefore be subject to orders which they have no part in making. Her will, if she has one, must give way before an alien will or, it may be, before a number of wills which are alien, not only to her but also to each other. And so long as that is true, German teachers, unlike Socrates, unlike the teachers of our American schools and colleges, have no political right to teach what they believe true.

5

This book has, I hope, succeeded in expressing the passionate devotion of one American citizen to the principle of the freedom of speech. And yet passions may blind us, as well as lead us. It will not do to pour out all our passion for freedom into such a cause as that which the First Amendment represents. When all that concerns our argument has been felt and said, the stark fact remains that the First Amendment is a negation. It protects. It forbids interference with something. And that protection can have value only as the "something" which is protected has value. What, we must ask, would be the use of giving to American citizens freedom to speak if they had nothing worth saying to say? Or—to state the principle less baldly—surely it is true that the protection of public discussion in our nation takes on an ever-increasing importance as the nation succeeds in so educating and informing its people that, in mind and will, they are able to think and act as self-governing citizens. And this means that far deeper and more significant than the demand for the freedom of speech is the demand for education, for the freeing of minds. These are not different demands. The one is a negative and external form of the other. We shall not understand the First Amendment unless we see that underlying it is the purpose that all the citizens of our self-governing society shall be "equally" educated.

I cannot, in these closing pages, discuss the methods, the successes and failures, of our national education—though my argument is only a fragment unless that is done. It is essential, however, to mention one typical failure which, since it has to do with the agencies of communication, falls within the field of our inquiry. The failure which I have in mind is that of the commercial radio.

When this new form of communication became available, there opened up before us the possibility that, as a people living a common life under a common agreement, we might communi-

cate with one another freely with regard to the values, the opportunities, the difficulties, the joys and sorrows, the hopes and
fears, the plans and purposes, of that common life. It seemed
possible that, amid all our differences, we might become a community of mutual understanding and of shared interests. It was
that hope which justified our making the radio "free," our giving
it the protection of the First Amendment.

But never was a human hope more bitterly disappointed. The
radio as it now operates among us is not free. Nor is it entitled
to the protection of the First Amendment. It is not engaged in
the task of enlarging and enriching human communication. It
is engaged in making money. And the First Amendment does
not intend to guarantee men freedom to say what some private
interest pays them to say for its own advantage. It intends only
to make men free to say what, as citizens, they think, what they
believe, about the general welfare.

As one utters these words of disappointment, one must grate-
fully acknowledge that there are, working in the radio business,
intelligent and devoted men who are fighting against the main
current. And their efforts are not wholly unavailing. But, in
spite of them, the total effect, as judged in terms of educational
value, is one of terrible destruction. The radio, as we now have
it, is not cultivating those qualities of taste, of reasoned judgment,
of integrity, of loyalty, of mutual understanding upon which the
enterprise of self-government depends. On the contrary, it is a
mighty force for breaking them down. It corrupts both our
morals and our intelligence. And that catastrophe is significant
for our inquiry, because it reveals how hollow may be the victories of the freedom of speech when our acceptance of the principle is merely formalistic. Misguided by that formalism we
Americans have given to the doctrine merely its negative meaning. We have used it for the protection of private, possessive interests with which it has no concern. It is misinterpretations such
as this which, in our use of the radio, the moving picture, the
newspaper and other forms of publication, are giving the name

"freedoms" to the most flagrant enslavements of our minds and wills.

6

Our final reflection brings us again face to face with that curious quality of paradox by which all interpretations of self-government are affected.

On the one hand, We, the People of the United States, are a body politic. Under the Constitution, we are agreed together that we will be, by corporate action, self-governed. We are agreed that as free men, politically equal, we alone will make the laws and that, as loyal citizens, equal before the laws, we will obey them. That is our social compact—the source both of our freedoms and of our obligations.

From that compact are derived the "just powers" of the government which we establish. That establishment does not mean that someone else, other than ourselves, has authority over us. It means that, in such ways as we may choose, we have taken authority over ourselves. It does not mean that we have lost our political freedom. It means that, by eternal vigilance, we are continually creating and securing it. So far as the compact is effective, we are not subservient to any Fuehrer or Dictator. But we are bound by obligations—obligations to one another and to the common cause in which we all share.

But, on the other side of the paradox, are the claims of an individualism which, when it becomes excessive, refuses to acknowledge the validity of political obligations. Men are, as they say, willing to work and sacrifice for the common good. But they are not willing that any political authority, even their own, shall require them to do so. Our blind and unthinking faith in the scheme of competitive strife which we so falsely call "the American Way of Life" blinds us to the meaning, and even to the existence, of the political agreement by which all our social institutions are inspired and directed.

How, then, shall we, the members of the body politic, become more clearly and effectively aware of our compact with one another? To bring that about is, I am sure, the primary task of American teaching. Our young women and men who enter into citizenship must learn what it means to be a member of a self-governing society. Our older citizens, if they have won that understanding, must be saved from losing it. It is the basic need of that understanding which finds partial and negative expression in the First Amendment. The guarding of the freedom of public discussion is a preliminary step in the unending attempt of our nation to be intelligent about its own purposes.

If, then, we seek to understand at its source that guarantee of the freedom of speech which the Constitution provides, I suggest that we pay heed to the sayings of two great teachers of freedom. Side by side with the Socratic "Know Thyself," let us place the saying of Epictetus, "The rulers of the state have said that only free men shall be educated; but Reason has said that only educated men shall be free." That is why, in the last resort, ". . . Congress shall make no law . . . abridging the freedom of speech."

PART TWO

THE FREEDOM OF THE ELECTORATE

INTRODUCTION

AS WE enter into the second phase of an interpretation of the First Amendment, we should, I think, read again the opening sentence of Chapter IV, "Reflections," which in 1948 brought the first phase of the discussion to its close. They are:

"No argument about principles is, I suppose, ever finished. But the argument of these lectures seems, to the writer of them, peculiarly incomplete. They constitute, it seems to me, not an inquiry, but only the beginning of an inquiry."

The attitude expressed by those words is, I am sure, justified by later experience. This renewal of our discussion should, therefore, begin by recognizing that the task of discovering the effective meaning of an abstract idea, such as that of Freedom, can never be finished. And that being true, it follows that we Americans have never fully known, and never will fully know, what we have in mind when we say that this nation of ours intends to be politically free. For example, as we read the words of the men who wrote the original Constitution and recommended its adoption, nothing is more certain than the fact that, though they were resolutely committed to principles, the meaning of those principles was, for them, controversial, uncertain, not clearly defined, and hence, in an important sense, not agreed upon.

In the Declaration of Independence and in the Preamble to the Constitution this nation pledged itself to the two assertions that "Governments derive their just powers from the consent of the governed" and that "We the People of the United States

. . . do ordain and establish this Constitution . . ." But the concrete question, "Who are The People of the United States, by whose consent and authority our government is maintained?" was never directly dealt with by the Constitutional Convention. On the contrary, that most important of all issues concerning Freedom was referred to the several states, to be dealt with by each of them in its own peculiar manner. And that action was taken with full knowledge that the states, in their differing ways, had always preferred, and would continue to prefer, the governing of the many by the few rather than the governing of all by themselves. In that sense the Constitutional Convention did not fully enact a program of self-government. Women were at that time excluded from the area of political dignity and independence. So, too, were slaves. Through the dominance of religious sects, here and there, heretics and non-believers were denied the vote. Persons whose possession of property fell below some prescribed level were held to be unfit for sharing in political action. Poll taxes were assessed with the same deadly effect. Non-Caucasians were regarded as "outsiders" and "aliens," subject to the laws but with no part in the making of them.

For the most part, these violations of the principles in which we Americans believe have now been formally cleared away by action of the several states and by the federal adoption of the Fifteenth and Ninetenth Amendments. Step by step, the will for Freedom has won its way toward conscious expression in action. However, with respect to exclusion "on account of race, color, or previous condition of servitude," though nearly a century has passed since the winning of the Civil War which was fought to ensure its abolition, the federal government is still relatively helpless in making that abolition effective.

In view of these successes and failures of our predecessors in the struggle to create and maintain the Constitution, it is well for us to realize that our own interpretation of its significance for the current problems of government is probably less clear and effective than was that of the forefathers in their dealing with the issues of their own time and situation. It is still true that for many reasons, ranging from external interference to inner ignorance and apathy, great masses of our people have little, if any, share in the governing of the nation. Only in a partial and formal way can we say that we are, as a whole nation, self-governed. Freedom is not, for us, a fact. It is a partly realized intention, which is contravened by many weaknesses of mind and will, by many self-deceptions, by many conflicting interests and their temptations. With respect to Freedom, as with respect to other human ideals and purposes, the unending task of our thinking is that of making more clear, to others and to ourselves, the goal toward which we are striving.

As I now invite the reader to consider attempts made between 1948 and 1958 to widen and deepen the earlier discussion of the First Amendment, two explanatory remarks may be useful and in order.

1

First, I wish it were possible to change the title of the original inquiry. That naming was dictated by the inaccurate and misleading American custom of using the phrase "Free Speech" to cover, by exclusion and inclusion, the list of those activities whose freedom the First Amendment protects. But the words "Freedom of Speech" are both too narrow and too wide in their reference to indicate the scope of the great charter of our political freedom. Many activities whose freedom the amendment protects are not "forms of speech." And there are many "forms of speech" about whose freedom the amendment has no concern. To fix our attention, as we commonly do, upon an individual "right to speak" is to lose sight of the essential issue. In a field in which the basic understanding of our plan of government is at stake, in which controversy rages and misunderstanding is easy, it is imperative that we have, so far as possible, a dependable working agreement as to the topic under consideration, as to the meaning of the words which we are using. I hope, therefore, that the reader will follow this argument as an attempt to understand not merely the "freedom to speak," but the "political freedom" which the Constitution establishes as the basis of any arrangement by which men may govern themselves, rather than submit to despotic control by others.

Second, the papers of Part Two do not, I think, express any divergence from the position taken in 1948. But there is in them a decided change of emphasis, already mentioned, which should be noted by way of introduction to the reading of them. The earlier statement rested chiefly upon the First Amendment and the Preamble. It placed most of its stress upon the fact that, in a free society, "the people" are the supreme source of all governing authority, prior in constitutional status to the legislative, executive, and judicial branches, which they have established. But the later statements, while holding fast to that ultimate principle, build their argument for freedom on the derivative fact that "the people" have not delegated all their authority, but have reserved to themselves a power of direct participation in the work of governing. By establishing themselves as an active and responsible "electorate" they have become a Fourth Branch of the government, co-ordinate with the other three branches. By virtue of that establishment they have "reserved" a freedom for their electoral activities with which the other branches are forbidden to interfere. It is that prohibition which the First Amendment expresses in its guarding of the freedom of speech, press, assembly, and petition.

The two provisions of the Constitution which bear most directly upon this inviolability of the powers of the Fourth Branch are:

(1) The Tenth Amendment, which reads: "The powers not delegated to the United States by the Constitution, nor pro-

hibited by it to the States, are reserved to the States respectively, or to the people."

(2) Article I, Section 2 (1), which reads: "The House of Representatives shall be composed of members chosen every second year by the people of the several States, and the electors in each State shall have the qualifications requisite for electors of the most numerous branch of the State Legislature."

It should perhaps be noted in passing that by amendment of the Constitution, Senators are also now chosen by direct popular voting. And in effect, the President is elected in the same way. As matter of sober fact, "We, the People," by our voting, do, or are called upon to do, a great deal of active and responsible governing. There are, then, four different agencies commissioned by the Constitution to carry on the governing of the United States—the Electoral, the Legislative, the Executive, and the Judicial. And the greatest among these governing equals is the Electoral.

2

The papers of Part Two will, I think, show that the theory which they advocate had been accepted and defended by the writers of the *Federalist* one hundred seventy years ago, even though the First and Tenth Amendments had not yet been enacted. When the Constitution-makers adopted Article 1, section 2 (1) they laid a foundation for political freedom in relation to which all other provisions of the Constitution are mere instruments and safeguards. Freedom cannot be assured merely by limiting the delegated powers of legislative, executive, and judicial agencies, and arranging that they shall check and counterbalance each other. Nor can it be created by establishing the popular custom of vigorous protest, through speech, press, assembly, and petition against governmental invasion of "The Rights of the People." These negative provisions are useful instruments of defense. But they are meaningless in relation to

Freedom unless, within the Constitution, there is another, a positive, enactment, whose interests they serve. That enactment assigns, or reserves, to the people a power to govern by voting, upon whose free, unlimited, and responsible exercise the entire structure of the Constitution rests. Epictetus is right. Men are politically free if, and only if, with adequate intelligence, with unremitting zeal for the nation's welfare, and by Constitutional authorization, they actively govern themselves. To be free does not mean to be well governed. It does not mean to be justly governed. It means to be self-governed.

What has just been said may, perhaps, be clarified by showing that it opposes a prevailing interpretation of political freedom which, arguing by slogans, powerfully affects our popular and judicial discussions of the relation between the people of the United States and the government of the United States.

That interpretation is commonly stated in the form of a rhetorical question. Its advocates seek to contrast our "free" political institutions with those of "non-free" nations and, as they do so, they commonly ask, "Are the people of the United States the servants of their government, or is the government a servant of the people?" And this question, with its strong emotional appeal, does not admit of a sensible answer because, as applied to a free nation, it is not a sensible question. It is primarily a verbal device by means of which we confusedly seek to dramatize the glories of our plan of government as contrasted with the vices of such non-free nations as Red Russia and Red China. Now the argument of this book is not immediately concerned with the truth or falsity of what we say about China or Russia. But it is deeply and directly concerned with the truth or falsity of what we say about ourselves.

The question of which we are speaking cannot be cleared of its slogan character unless we recognize that, under the Constitution, "the people" and "the government" have three different relations to each other, rather than only one. What, then, are those relations?

The first of them is indicated by the Preamble when it says, "We the People of the United States . . . do ordain and establish this Constitution . . ." Those words tell us that the people of the United States are a sovereign government. In them all authority to govern this nation is vested. Through the adoption of the Constitution we Americans are a self-governing body-politic. We are the government. And this means that people and government are neither master nor servant of each other. They *are* each other.

But a second relation arises from two practical necessities. First, the body-politic can do its work, in so complex a society as ours, only by delegating—though not abdicating—certain of its governing powers to legislative, executive, and judicial agencies. In a subordinate capacity, those agencies are commonly spoken of as being "the government of the United States."

But on the other hand, an even greater practical necessity requires, as we have already noted, that these three subordinate agencies shall be kept permanently and decisively under the active control of the voting body-politic. "We the people" have reserved powers to ourselves, as well as delegated them. And unless we exercise vigorously, intelligently, and with scrupulous regard for the common good, the reserved power of "election," the machinery of representative government will drive toward enslavement rather than toward freedom.

In this second Constitutional relationship, then, the voters of the nation, acting as a corporate body, are the "masters," and the legislative, executive, and judicial government is their "servant."

But a third Constitutional relationship between people and government arises from the provision of our "Social Compact" that all people within our borders, whether they are voters or not, shall be subject to the laws.

Those laws are enacted, administered, and interpreted in virtue of the powers which we have delegated to our agents. In every kind of activity, except the religious and the electoral, which are protected by the First Amendment, individuals and groups are, in defined ways, under the legal control of our representatives. In the interest of the public welfare, each of us may be deprived of life, liberty, or property at their discretion. We may be told what we must do, what we are forbidden to do. In these negative aspects of the law we are, all alike, "servants" or "subjects" of a "government" which we, acting in our corporate capacity as a ruling body, have authorized to be, in all our non-ruling activities, a "master" whom we must obey.

Are we then servants of our government or masters over it? As the meanings of the terms "government" and "people" change, that is not one question, but three different questions. And, in answer to these three different questions, three different assertions may be validly made. First, the people of the United States are the government: They govern themselves. Second, they are the masters of the government, since the legislative, executive, and judicial agencies are their subordinates. But, third, they are also the servants of the government, subject to laws, and required to obey them. And the use of slogans which would require us to choose one of these statements and, hence, to reject the others, is unworthy of women and men who are members of a free society.

The papers of Part Two are attempts to make clear the Constitutional relations which, by such ambiguities and tricks, we constantly distort and obscure. Our attempts to understand the American plan of government may fail. But the task is one in which every loyal citizen should be persistently engaged.

THE CONGRESS AND THE PEOPLE

A. The Limitations of Congressional Authority (1953)

IN HIS concurring opinion in the Dennis case, my life-long friend, Mr. Justice Frankfurter, used an argument which seems to me to sap the very foundations of our American political freedom. He quotes as authoritative the majority decision in Robertson v. Baldwin, rendered in 1897, which says—

The law is perfectly well settled that the first ten amendments to the Constitution, commonly known as the Bill of Rights, were not intended to lay down any novel principles of government, but simply to embody certain guaranties and immunities which we had inherited from our English ancestors, and which had from time immemorial been subject to certain well-recognized exceptions arising from the necessities of the case. In incorporating these principles into the fundamental law there was no intent of disregarding the exceptions which continued to be recognized as if they had been formally expressed.

In comment on this, Justice Frankfurter adds—

"That this represents the authentic view of the Bill of Rights and the spirit in which it must be construed has been recognized again and again in cases that have come here within the last fifty years."

Is it true that our Bill of Rights "laid down no novel principles of government"? Are we to believe that the American Revolution had no revolutionary *political* significance? Was the dictum, "Congress shall make no law respecting an establishment of religion," etc. "inherited from our *English* ancestors?" With respect to certain items in the Bill of Rights, the denial of novelty is, of course, valid. Such rights as habeas corpus, due process, fair trial, freedom of contract, security from unreasonable searches and seizures, and so on, had long been fought for, and in some measure won, in Britain and the Colonies. It could fairly be said of them that "no novel principles had been laid down." But to say that the relation between the people and the legislature was now, in principle, as it had been before, is to miss the meaning, not only of the First Amendment, but of the Constitution as a whole. Before we accept a doctrine so monstrous in its destruction of our freedom I ask you to examine with me two sets of opinions held by men of high repute in political theory which sharply reject this "authentic" doctrine. The first is taken from the writings of James Madison and Alexander Hamilton in the *Federalist*. The second is found in a dissent by Justice Harlan, attacking the decision in which the "authentic view" was formulated.

First, then, let us listen to Madison and Hamilton in the *Federalist*. Throughout their arguments there runs a subtle and powerful insistence on the need of limiting legislative power. And the unfailing purpose of their inquiry is to find ways of guarding the political freedom of the people from invasion by the lawmakers. It is, of course, recognized that Congress has authority to enact laws which the people must obey. In this legal sense, the people are dependent on, are subject to, the legislature. But with respect to political authority, that relation is reversed. If men are to be self-governing, as the Constitution intends, they must exercise an effective control over those legislators who make the laws which they are called upon to obey. Politically, they must govern those who, legally, govern them. This double relationship Hamilton brilliantly describes in the words—

"It is one thing to be subject to the laws, and another to be dependent on the legislative body. The first comports with, the last violates the fundamental principles of good government, and, whatever may be the form of the Constitution, unites all power in the same hands."

With hard, incisive logic, Hamilton demonstrates the necessity that the legislature be kept subject to the will of a free people. It is chiefly the legislature, he tells us, which threatens to usurp the authority of the people. And again, he says, "it is against the enterprising ambition of this department that the people ought to indulge all their jealousy and exhaust all their precautions." And the Constitution, he assures us, has carefully taken those precautions. By direct vote, the people will elect their representatives. Elections will be for terms brief enough to ensure active and continuous popular control. Representatives will have no powers other than those specifically delegated to them. A general legislative power would contravene the basic principles of the system. Politically, the law-makers are, and must be, the servants of the people.

Hamilton's argument to this effect reaches its culmination when in number 84 of the series, he deals with the accusation that the new Constitution does not provide a Bill of Rights. The plan of the Convention, he declares, does not need a Bill of Rights. It does far more to protect the freedom of the people from legislative usurpation than could possibly be done by appending a Bill of Rights to a Constitution which, having neglected those rights, would have need of such an appendage. The defences of our freedom, he declares, are embedded in the very structure of the Constitution itself. Whoever attacks that freedom is attacking, not an addendum to the Constitution, but the living spirit of the whole.

Over and over again, he reiterates that assertion. I can give here only one of his statements—

The truth is, after all the declamations we have heard, that the Constitution is itself, in every rational sense, and to every useful purpose, a Bill of Rights. . . . Is it one object of a bill of rights to declare and specify the political privileges of the citizens in the structure and administration of the government? This is done in the most ample and precise manner in the plan of the convention, comprehending various precautions for the public security, which are not to be found in any of the State constitutions. Is another object of a bill of rights to define certain immunities and modes of proceeding, which are relative to personal and private concerns? This we have seen has also been attended to, in a variety of cases, in the same plan. Adverting therefore to the substantial meaning of a bill of rights it is absurd to allege that it is not to be found in the work of the convention.

If Hamilton is right, as I think he is, the assertion that the American Constitution established no "novel principles of government" is a patent and disastrous absurdity—an absurdity in which our current suppressions of political freedom find their source. Over and over again Madison and Hamilton proclaim the faith which that heresy denies. In number 14, Madison writes—

Had no important step been taken by the leaders of the Revolution for which a precedent could not be discovered, no government established of which an exact model did not present itself, the people of the United States might, at this moment, have been numbered among the melancholy victims of misguided councils, must at best have been labouring under the weight of those forms which have crushed the liberties of the rest of mankind. Happily for America, happily, we trust, for the whole human race, they pursued a new and more noble course. They accomplished a revolution which has no parallel in the annals of human society. They reared the fabrics of governments which have no model on the face of the globe.

The same unequivocal rejection of the "authentic view" of the contemporary Court is strongly urged by Justice Harlan in his dissent from the decision out of which that view is now quoted.

He discards as wholly invalid the inference that because the British Parliament could make exceptions to a principle, the Congress of the United States could do the same.

"Nor, I submit," he says, "is any light thrown upon the present question by the history of legislation in Great Britain. The powers of the British Parliament furnish no test for the powers that may be exercised by the Congress of the United States."

In support of that opinion he calls upon James Bryce who, in *The American Commonwealth,* tells how fundamentally the principles of the Constitution have departed from the principles of the British system. Parliament, according to Bryce, had unlimited power. It could, he says, "abolish when it pleases every institution in the country, the Crown, the House of Lords, the Established Church, the House of Commons, Parliament itself."

By contrast with the original and unlimited authority of the British legislature, Justice Harlan insists that the powers of the American Congress are derivative and subordinate, as well as limited and specific. The distinctive feature of our Constitution is that it is established not by the legislature but by the people.

"No such powers," he says, "have been given to or can be exercised by any legislative body under the American system. . . . The authority for the exercise of power by the Congress must be found in the Constitution. Whatever it does in excess of the powers granted to it, or in violation of the supreme law of the land, is a nullity, and may be so treated by any person."

He, therefore, deplores a decision in which "the clear reading of a constitutional provision relating to the liberty of man is departed from in deference to what is called usage which has existed, for the most part, in monarchical and despotic governments."

Here, then, as we Americans consider our freedom, is the principle on which we may take our stand with Madison and Hamilton and Harlan. Insofar as we are true to the Constitution, we are not living under "monarchical or despotic governments."

Our legislature has no authority to exercise control over our political freedom. The intent of the Constitution is that, politically, we shall be governed by no one but ourselves. We are not, then, a subject people begging or fighting for such limited privileges and powers as may be grudgingly granted to us by a sovereign legislature. We are the sovereign and the legislature is our agent. And as we play our sovereign role in what Hamilton calls "the structure and administration of the government," that agent has no authority whatever to interfere with the freedom of our governing. As we go about that work neither Congress nor any committee of Congress may use force upon us to drive us toward this public policy or that, or away from this public policy or that. A legislative committee which asks the question, "Are you a Republican?" or "Are you a Communist?"—accompanying the question with the threat of harm or disrepute if the answer is this rather than that—stands in contempt of the sovereign people to whom it owes submission. In the words of Justice Harlan, such action "is a nullity, and may be so treated by any person." We Americans, acting as free citizens, may make mistakes; we may be selfish or stupid or negligent. But in the field of political opinion or expression or affiliation we cannot commit a punishable crime for the reason that, in that field, the law-makers have no authority to legislate a crime into existence.

At this final point, my lawyer friends will, I know, say to me, "Don't you know that the law is what the Supreme Court says it is?" And to that I answer in closing, "Yes, I know that the law today is what today the Court says it is. But you see I am hoping that tomorrow the members of the Court will read again from Madison and Hamilton and Harlan. Perhaps tomorrow they will change their minds. But today I would say to them that the Supreme Court of the last forty years, more than any other agency or person in our society, must be held responsible for the destruction of those Constitutional principles which that court is commissioned to interpret and to defend."

B. *Testimony on the Meaning of the First Amendment*

(Testimony presented November 14, 1955, to the Hennings Senate Sub-Committee on Constitutional Rights, authorized by the Senate Committee on the Judiciary.)

Mr. Chairman and Members of the Committee:

I deeply appreciate your courtesy in asking me to join with you in an attempt to define the meaning of the words, "Congress shall make no law . . . abridging the freedom of speech, or of the press; or the right of the people peaceably to assemble, and to petition the government for a redress of grievances." Whatever those words may mean, they go directly to the heart of our American plan of government. If we can understand them we can know what, as a self-governing nation, we are trying to be and to do. Insofar as we do not understand them, we are in grave danger of blocking our own purposes, of denying our own beliefs.

1

It may clarify my own part in our conference if I tell you at once my opinion concerning this much-debated subject. The First Amendment seems to me to be a very uncompromising statement. It admits of no exceptions. It tells us that the Congress and, by implication, all other agencies of the government are denied any authority whatever to limit the political freedom of the citizens of the United States. It declares that with respect to political belief, political discussion, political advocacy, political planning, our citizens are sovereign, and the Congress is their subordinate agent. That agent is authorized, under strong safeguards against the abuse of its power, to limit the freedom of men as they go about the management of their private, their non-political, affairs. But the same men, as they endeavor to meet the public responsibilities of citizenship in a free society, are in a vital sense, which is not easy to define, beyond the reach of legislative control. Our common task, as we talk together today, is to determine what that sense is.

Mr. Chairman, in view of your courtesy to me, I hope you will not find me discourteous when I suggest that the Congress is a subordinate branch of the government of the United States. In saying this I am simply repeating in less passionate words what was said by the writers of the *Federalist* papers when, a century and three-quarters ago, they explained the meaning of the proposed Constitution to a body politic which seemed very reluctant to adopt it. Over and over again the writers of those papers declared that the Constitutional Convention had given to the people adequate protection against a much-feared tyranny of the legislature. In one of the most brilliant statements ever written about the Constitution, the *Federalist* says—

It is one thing to be subject to the laws, and another to be dependent on the legislative body. The first comports with, the last violates, the fundamental principles of good government, and, whatever may be the forms of the Constitution, unites all power in the same hands. (No. 71)

It is chiefly the legislature, the *Federalist* insists, which threatens to usurp the governing powers of the people. In words which unfortunately have some relevance today, it declares that "it is against the enterprising ambition of this department that the people ought to indulge their jealousy and exhaust all their precautions." And, further, the hesitant people were assured that the Convention, having recognized this danger, had devised adequate protections against it. The representatives, it was provided, would be elected by vote of the people. Elections would be for terms brief enough to ensure active and continuous popular control. The legislature would have no law-making authority other than those limited powers specifically delegated to it. A general legislative power to act for the security and welfare of the nation was denied on the ground that it would destroy the basic postulate of popular self-government on which the Constitution rests.

As the *Federalist* thus describes, with insight and accuracy, the Constitutional defenses of the freedom of the people against legislative invasion, it is not speaking of that freedom as an "individual right" which is bestowed upon the citizens by action of the legislature. Nor is the principle of the freedom of speech derived from a law of Nature or of Reason in the abstract. As it stands in the Constitution, it is an expression of the basic American political agreement that, in the last resort, the people of the United States shall govern themselves. To find its meaning, therefore, we must dig down to the very foundations of the self-governing process. And what we shall there find is the fact that when men govern themselves, it is they—and no one else—who must pass judgment upon public policies. And that means that in our popular discussions, unwise ideas must have a hearing as well as wise ones, dangerous ideas as well as safe, un-American as well as American. Just so far as, at any point, the citizens who are to decide issues are denied acquaintance with information or opinion or doubt or disbelief or criticism which is relevant to those issues, just so far the result must be ill-considered, ill-balanced planning for the general good. It is that mutilation of the thinking process of the community against which the First Amendment is directed. That provision neither the Legislature, nor the Executive, nor the Judiciary, nor all of them acting together, has authority to nullify. We Americans have, together, decided to be politically free.

2

Mr. Chairman, I have now stated for your consideration the thesis that the First Amendment is not "open to exceptions"; that our American "freedom of speech" is not, on any grounds whatever, subject to abridgment by the representatives of the people. May I next try to answer two arguments which are commonly brought against that thesis in the courts and in the wider circle of popular discussion?

The first objection rests upon the supposition that freedom of speech may on occasion threaten the security of the nation. And when these two legitimate national interests are in conflict, the government, it is said, must strike a balance between them. And that means that the First Amendment must at times yield ground. The freedom of speech must be abridged in order that the national order and safety may be secured.

In the courts of the United States, many diverse opinions have asserted that "balancing" doctrine. One of these, often quoted, reads as follows:

> To preserve its independence, and give security against foreign aggression and encroachment, is the highest duty of every nation, and to attain these ends nearly all other considerations are to be subordinated. It matters not in what form such aggression comes. . . . The government, possessing the powers which are to be exercised for protection and security, is clothed with authority to determine the occasion on which the powers shall be brought forth.

That opinion tells us that the "government" of the United States has unlimited authority to provide for the security of the nation, as it may seem necessary and wise. It tells us, therefore, that constitutionally, the government which has created the defenses of political freedom may break down those defenses. We, the people, who have enacted the First Amendment, may by agreed-upon procedure modify or annul that amendment. And, since we are, as a government, a sovereign nation, I do not see how any of these assertions can be doubted or denied. We Americans, as a body-politic, may destroy or limit our freedom whenever we choose. But what bearing has that statement upon the authority of Congress to interfere with the provisions of the First Amendment? Congress is not the government. It is only one of four branches to each of which the people have denied specific and limited powers as well as delegated such powers. And in the

case before us, the words, "Congress shall make no law . . .
abridging the freedom of speech," give plain evidence that, so
far as Congress is concerned, the power to limit our political
freedom has been explicitly denied.

There is, I am sure, a radical error in the theory that the task
of "balancing" the conflicting claims of security and freedom has
been delegated to Congress. It is the failure to recognize that the
balancing in question was carefully done when, one hundred
seventy years ago, the Constitution was adopted and quickly
amended. The men who wrote the text of that Constitution knew,
quite as well as we do, that the program of political freedom is
a dangerous one. They could foresee that, as the nation traveled
the ways of self-government, the freedom of speech would often be
used irresponsibly and unwisely, especially in times of war or
near-war, and that such talking might have serious consequences
for the national safety.

They knew, too, that a large section of the voting population
was hostile to the forms of government which were then being
adopted. And, further, they had every reason to expect that in a
changing world, new dissatisfactions would arise and might in
times of stress break out into open and passionate disaffection. All
these considerations, I am saying, were as clearly and as disturb-
ingly present to their minds as they are to our minds today. And
because of them, the First Amendment might have been written,
not as it is, but as the Courts of the United States have re-written
it in the war-maddened years since 1919. The Amendment might
have said, "Except in times and situations involving 'clear and
present danger' to the national security, Congress shall make no
law abridging the freedom of speech." Or it might have read,
"Only when, in the judgment of the legislature, the interests of
order and security render such action advisable shall Congress
abridge the freedom of speech." But the writers of the Amendment did not adopt either of these phrasings or anything like
them. Perhaps a minor reason for their decision was the practical
certainty that the Constitution, if presented in that form, would

have failed of adoption. But more important than such question-
able historical speculation are two reasons which are as valid
today as they were when the Amendment was decreed.

First, our doctrine of political freedom is not a visionary
abstraction. It is a belief which is based in long and bitter experience, which is thought out by shrewd intelligence. It is the sober
conviction that, in a society pledged to self-government, it is never
true that, in the long run, the security of the nation is endangered
by the freedom of the people. Whatever may be the immediate
gains and losses, the dangers to our safety arising from political
suppression are always greater than the dangers to that safety
arising from political freedom. Suppression is always foolish.
Freedom is always wise. That is the faith, the experimental faith,
by which we Americans have undertaken to live. If we, the
citizens of today, cannot shake ourselves free from the hysteria
which blinds us to that faith, there is little hope for peace and
security, either at home or abroad.

Second, the re-writing of the First Amendment which authorizes the legislature to balance security against freedom denies not
merely some minor phase of the amendment but its essential
purpose and meaning. Whenever, in our Western civilization,
"inquisitors" have sought to justify their acts of suppression, they
have given plausibility to their claims only by appealing to the
necessity of guarding the public safety. It is that appeal which
the First Amendment intended, and intends, to outlaw. Speaking
to the legislature, it says, "When times of danger come upon the
nation, you will be strongly tempted, and urged by popular pressure, to resort to practices of suppression such as those allowed by
societies unlike our own in which men do not govern themselves.
You are hereby forbidden to do so. This nation of ours intends to
be free. 'Congress shall make no law . . . abridging the freedom
of speech.'"

The second objection which must be met by one who asserts
the unconditional freedom of speech rests upon the well-known
fact that there are countless human situations in which, under the

Constitution, this or that kind of speaking may be limited or forbidden by legislative action. Some of these cases have been listed by the courts in vague and varying ways. Thus libels, blasphemies, attacks upon public morals or private reputation have been held punishable. So too, we are told that "counselling a murder" may be a criminal act, or "falsely shouting fire in a theatre, and causing a panic." "Offensive" or "provocative" speech has been denied legislative immunity. "Contempt of court," shown by the use of speech or by refusal to speak, may give basis for prosecution. Utterances which cause a riot or which "incite" to it may be subject to the same legal condemnation. And this listing of legitimate legislative abridgments of speech could be continued indefinitely. Their number is legion.

In view of these undoubted facts, the objection which we must now try to meet can be simply stated. In all these cases, it says, inasmuch as speaking is abridged, "exceptions" are made to the First Amendment. The Amendment is thus shown to be, in general, "open to exceptions." And from this it follows that there is no reason why a legislature which has authority to guard the public safety should be debarred from making an "exception" when faced by the threat of national danger.

Now the validity of that argument rests upon the assumed major premise that whenever, in any way, limits are set to the speaking of an individual, an "exception" is made to the First Amendment. But that premise is clearly false. It could be justified only if it were shown that the Amendment intends to forbid every form of governmental control over the act of speaking. Is that its intention? Nothing could be further from the truth. May I draw an example from our own present activities in this room? You and I are here talking about freedom within limits defined by the Senate. I am allowed to speak only because you have invited me to do so. And just now everyone else is denied that privilege. But further, you have assigned me a topic to which my remarks must be relevant. Your schedule, too, acting with generosity, fixes a time within which my remarks must be made. In a word, my speaking, though "free" in the First Amendment sense, is abridged in many ways. But your speaking, too, is controlled by rules of procedure. You may, of course, differ in opinion from what I am saying. To that freedom there are no limits. But unless the chairman intervenes, you are not allowed to express that difference by open speech until I have finished my reading. In a word, both you and I are under control as to what we may say and when and how we may say it. Shall we say, then, that this conference, which studies the principle of free speech, is itself making "exceptions" to that principle? I do not think so. Speech, as a form of human action, is subject to regulation in exactly the same sense as is walking, or lighting a fire, or shooting a gun. To interpret the First Amendment as forbidding such regulation is to so misconceive its meaning as to reduce it to nonsense.

The principle here at issue was effectively, though not clearly, stated by Mr. Justice Holmes when, in the *Frohwerk* case, he said—

The First Amendment, while prohibiting legislation against free speech as such, cannot have been, and obviously was not, intended to give immunity to every form of language. . . . We venture to believe that neither Hamilton nor Madison, nor any other competent person, ever supposed that to make criminal the counselling of a murder would be an unconstitutional interference with free speech.

Those words of the great Justice, by denying that the First Amendment intends to forbid such abridgments of speech as the punishing of incitement to murder, seem to me to nullify completely the supposed evidence that the amendment is "open to exceptions." They show conclusively the falsity of the "exception" theory which has been used by the courts to give basis for the "danger" theory of legislative authority to abridge our political freedom. If, then, the "danger" theory is to stand it must stand on its own feet. And those feet, if my earlier argument is valid, seem to be made of clay.

3

Mr. Chairman, in the first section of this paper I spoke of the negative fact that the First Amendment forbids the legislature to limit the political freedom of the people. May I now, surveying the same ground from its positive side, discuss with you the active powers and responsibilities of free citizens, as these are described or taken for granted in the general structure of the Constitution as a whole? If I am not mistaken, we shall find here the reasons why the words of the great proclamation are so absolute, so uncompromising, so resistant of modification or exception.

The purpose of the Constitution is, as we all know, to define and allocate powers for the governing of the nation. To that end, three special governing agencies are set up, and to each of them are delegated such specific powers as are needed for doing its part of the work.

Now that program rests upon a clear distinction between the political body which delegates powers and the political bodies— Legislative, Executive, and Judicial—to which powers are delegated. It presupposes, on the one hand, a supreme governing agency to which, originally, all authority belongs. It specifies, on the other hand, subordinate agencies to which partial delegations of authority are made. What, then, is the working relation between the supreme agency and its subordinates? Only as we answer that question shall we find the positive meaning of the First Amendment.

First of all, then, what is the supreme governing agency of this nation? In its opening statement the Constitution answers that question. "We, the People of the United States," it declares, "do ordain and establish this Constitution . . ." Those are revolutionary words which define the freedom which is guaranteed by the First Amendment. They mark off our government from every form of despotic polity. The legal powers of the people of the United States are not granted to them by some one else—by kings or barons or priests, by legislators or executives or judges.

All political authority, whether delegated or not, belongs, constitutionally, to us. If any one else has political authority, we are lending it to him. We, the people, are supreme in our own right. We are governed, directly or indirectly, only by ourselves.

But now what have we, the people, in our establishing of the Constitution, done with the powers which thus inhere in us? Some of them we have delegated. But there is one power, at least, which we have not delegated, which we have kept in our own hands, for our own direct exercise. Article 1, (2), authorizes the people, in their capacity as "electors," to choose their representatives. And that means that we, the people, in a vital sense, do actively govern those who, by other delegated powers, govern us. In the midst of all our assigning of powers to legislative, executive, and judicial bodies, we have jealously kept for ourselves the most fundamental of all powers. It is the power of voting, of choosing by joint action, those representatives to whom certain of our powers are entrusted. In the view of the Constitution, then, we the people are not only the supreme agency. We are also, politically, an active electorate—a Fourth, or perhaps better, a First Branch which, through its reserved power, governs at the polls. That is the essential meaning of the statement that we Americans are, in actual practice, politically a free people. Our First Amendment freedom is not merely an aspiration. It is an arrangement made by women and men who vote freely and, by voting, govern the nation. That is the responsibility, the opportunity, which the Constitution assigns to us, however slackly and negligently we may at times have exercised our power.

It follows from what has just been said that under the Constitution, we Americans are politically free only insofar as our voting is free. But to get the full meaning of that statement we must examine more closely what men are doing when they vote, and how they do it.

The most obvious feature of activity at the polls is the choosing among candidates for office. But under our election procedures, with their party platforms and public meetings, with the turmoil and passion of partisan debate, the voters are also considering and deciding about issues of public policy. They are thinking. As we vote we do more than elect men to represent us. We also judge the wisdom or folly of suggested measures. We plan for the welfare of the nation. Now it is these "judging" activities of the governing people which the First Amendment protects by its guarantees of freedom from legislative interference. Because, as self-governing women and men, we the people have work to do for the general welfare, we make two demands. First, our judging of public issues, whether done separately or in groups, must be free and independent—must be our own. It must be done by us and by no one else. And second, we must be equally free and independent in expressing, at the polls, the conclusions, the beliefs, to which our judging has brought us. Censorship over our thinking, duress over our voting, are alike forbidden by the First Amendment. A legislative body, or any other body which, in any way, practices such censorship or duress, stands in "contempt" of the sovereign people of the United States.

But, further, what more specifically are the judging activities with which censorship and duress attempt to interfere? What are the intellectual processes by which free men govern a nation, which therefore must be protected from any external interference? They seem to be of three kinds.

First, as we try to "make up our minds" on issues which affect the general welfare, we commonly—though not commonly enough—read the printed records of the thinking and believing which other men have done in relation to those issues. Those records are found in documents and newspapers, in works of art of many kinds. And all this vast array of idea and fact, of science and fiction, of poetry and prose, of belief and doubt, of appreciation and purpose, of information and argument, the voter may find ready to help him in making up his mind.

Second, we electors do our thinking, not only by individual reading and reflection, but also in the active associations of private or public discussion. We think together, as well as apart.

And in this field, by the group action of congenial minds, by the controversies of opposing minds, we form parties, adopt platforms, conduct campaigns, hold meetings, in order that this or that set of ideas may prevail, in order that that measure or this may be defeated.

And third, when election day finally comes, the voter, having presumably made up his mind, must now express it by his ballot. Behind the canvas curtain, alone and independent, he renders his decision. He acts as sovereign, one of the governors of his country. However slack may be our practice, that, in theory, is our freedom.

What, then, as seen against this Constitutional background, is the purpose of the First Amendment, as it stands guard over our freedom? That purpose is to see to it that in none of these three activities of judging shall the voter be robbed, by action of other, subordinate branches of the government, of the responsibility, the power, the authority, which are his under the Constitution. What shall be read? What he himself decides to read. With whom shall he associate in political advocacy? With those with whom he chooses to associate. Whom shall he oppose? Those with whom he disagrees. Shall any branch of the government attempt to control his opinions or his vote, to drive him by duress or intimidation into believing or voting this way or that? To do this is to violate the Constitution at its very source. We, the people of the United States, are self-governing. That is what our freedom means.

4

Mr. Chairman, this interpretation of the First Amendment which I have tried to give is, of necessity, very abstract. May I, therefore, give some more specific examples of its meaning at this point or that?

First, when we speak of the Amendment as guarding the freedom to hear and to read, the principle applies not only to the speaking or writing of our own citizens but also to the writing or speaking of every one whom a citizen, at his own discretion, may choose to hear or to read. And this means that unhindered expression must be open to non-citizens, to resident aliens, to writers and speakers of other nations, to anyone, past or present, who has something to say which may have significance for a citizen who is thinking of the welfare of this nation. The Bible, the Koran, Plato, Adam Smith, Joseph Stalin, Gandhi, may be published and read in the United States, not because they have, or had, a right to be published here, but because we, the citizen-voters, have authority, have legal power, to decide what we will read, what we will think about. With the exercise of that "reserved" power, all "delegated" powers are, by the Constitution, forbidden to interfere.

Second, in the field of public discussion, when citizens and their fellow thinkers "peaceably assemble" to listen to a speaker, whether he be American or foreign, conservative or radical, safe or dangerous, the First Amendment is not, in the first instance, concerned with the "right" of the speaker to say this or that. It is concerned with the authority of the hearers to meet together, to discuss, and to hear discussed by speakers of their own choice, whatever they may deem worthy of their consideration.

Third, the same freedom from attempts at duress is guaranteed to every citizen as he makes up his mind, chooses his party, and finally casts his vote. During that process, no governing body may use force upon him, may try to drive him or lure him toward this decision or that, or away from this decision or that. And for that reason, no subordinate agency of the government has authority to ask, under compulsion to answer, what a citizen's political commitments are. The question, "Are you a Republican?" or "Are you a Communist?", when accompanied by the threat of harmful or degrading consequences if an answer is refused, or if the answer is this rather than that, is an intolerable invasion of the "reserved powers" of the governing people. And the freedom thus protected does not rest upon the Fifth Amendment "right" of one who is governed to avoid self-incrimination. It expresses the constitutional authority, the legal power, of one who governs to make up his own mind without fear or favor, with the independence and freedom in which self-government consists.

And fourth, for the same reason, our First Amendment freedom forbids that any citizen be required under threat of penalty to take an oath, or make an affirmation as to beliefs which he holds or rejects. Every citizen, it is true, may be required, and should be required, to pledge loyalty, and to practice loyalty, to the nation. He must agree to support the Constitution. But he may never be required to *believe* in the Constitution. His loyalty may never be tested on grounds of adherence to, or rejection of, any *belief*. Loyalty does not imply conformity of opinion. Every citizen of the United States has Constitutional authority to approve or to condemn any laws enacted by the Legislature, any actions taken by the Executive, any decisions rendered by the Judiciary, any principles established by the Constitution. All these enactments which, as men who are governed, we must obey, are subject to our approval or disapproval, as we govern. With respect to all of them, we, who are free men, are sovereign. We are "The People." We govern the United States.

5

Mr. Chairman, I have tried to state and defend the assertion that Constitutional guarantee of political freedom is not "open to exceptions." Judgment upon the theoretical validity of that position I now leave in your hands.

But as between conflicting views of the First Amendment, there is also a practical question of efficiency. May I, in closing, speaking with the tentativeness becoming to a non-lawyer, offer three suggestions as to the working basis on which decisions about political freedom should rest?

First, the experience of the courts since 1919 seems to me to show that, as a procedural device for distinguishing forms of speech and writing and assembly which the Amendment does protect from those which it does not protect, the "clear and present danger" test has failed to work. Its basic practical defect is that no one has been able to give it dependable, or even assignable, meaning. Case by case, opinion by opinion, it has shifted back and forth with a variability of meaning which reveals its complete lack of Constitutional basis. In his opinion confirming the conviction of Eugene Dennis and others for violation of the Smith Act, Judge Learned Hand reviewed the long series of judicial attempts to give to the words "clear and present" a usable meaning. His conclusion reads, in part, as follows:

The phrase "clear and present danger" . . . is a way to describe a penumbra of occasions, even the outskirts of which are indefinable, but within which, as is so often the case, the courts must find their way as they can. In each case they must ask whether the gravity of the "evil," discounted by its improbability, justifies such an invasion of free speech as is necessary to avoid the danger.

And to this bewildering interpretation of the words, "clear and present," he adds:

That is a test in whose application the utmost differences of opinion have constantly arisen, even in the Supreme Court. Obviously it would be impossible to draft a statute which should attempt to prescribe a rule for each occasion; and it follows, as we have said, either that the Act is definite enough as it stands, or that it is practically impossible to deal with such conduct in general terms.

Those words, coming from the penetrating and powerful mind of Learned Hand, show how intolerable it is that the most precious, most fundamental, value in the American plan of government should depend, for its defense, upon a phrase which not only has no warrant in the Constitution but has no dependable meaning, either for a man accused of crime or for the attorneys who prosecute or defend him or for the courts which judge him. That phrase does not do its work. We need to make a fresh start in our interpreting of the words which protect our political freedom.

Second, as we seek for a better test, it is of course true that no legal device can transform the making of decisions about freedom into a merely routine application of an abstract principle. Self-government is a complicated business. And yet, the "no-exception" view which I have offered seems to me to promise a more stable and understandable basis for judicial decision than does the 1919 doctrine which the courts have been trying to follow. For example, the most troublesome issue which now confronts our courts and our people is that of the speech and writing and assembling of persons who find, or think they find, radical defects in our form of government, and who devise and advocate plans by means of which another form might be substituted for it. And the practical question is, "How far, and in what respects, are such revolutionary planning and advocacy protected by the First Amendment?"

It is, of course, understood that if such persons or groups proceed to forceful or violent action, or even to overt preparation for such action, against the government, the First Amendment offers them, in that respect, no protection. Its interest is limited to the freedom of judgment-making—of inquiry and belief and conference and persuasion and planning and advocacy. It does not protect either overt action or incitement to such action. It is concerned only with those political activities by which, under the Constitution, free men govern themselves.

From what has just been said it follows that, so far as speech and writing are concerned, the distinction upon which the application of the First Amendment rests is that between "advocacy of action" and "incitement to action." To advocacy the amendment guarantees freedom, no matter what may be advocated. To incitement, on the other hand, the amendment guarantees nothing whatever.

This distinction was sharply drawn by Justice Brandeis when, in the *Whitney* case, he said—

Every denunciation of existing law tends in some measure to increase the probability that there will be violations of it. Condonation of a breach enhances the probability. Propagation of the criminal state of mind by teaching syndicalism increases it. Advocacy of law-breaking heightens it still further. But even advocacy of violation, however reprehensible morally, is not a justification for denying free speech where the advocacy falls short of incitement and there is nothing to indicate that the advocacy would be immediately acted on.

Those words, I think, point the way which decisions about our political freedom can, and should, follow. An incitement, I take it, is an utterance so related to a specific overt act that it may be regarded and treated as a part of the doing of the act itself, if the act is done. Its control, therefore, falls within the jurisdiction of the legislature. An advocacy, on the other hand, even up to the limit of arguing and planning for the violent overthrow of the existing form of government, is one of those opinion-forming, judgment-making expressions which free men need to utter and to hear as citizens responsible for the governing of the nation. If men are not free to ask and to answer the question, "Shall the present form of our government be maintained or changed?"; if, when that question is asked, the two sides of the issue are not equally open for consideration, for advocacy, and for adoption, then it is impossible to speak of our government as established by the free choice of a self-governing people. It is not enough to say that the people of the United States were free one hundred seventy years ago. The First Amendment requires, simply and without equivocation, that they be free now.

Third, and finally, if we say, as this paper has urged, that in many situations, speech and writing and assembly may be controlled by legislative action, we must also say that such control may never be based on the ground of disagreement with opinions held or expressed. No belief or advocacy may be denied freedom if, in the same situation, opposing beliefs or advocacies are granted that freedom.

If then, on any occasion in the United States, it is allowable to say that the Constitution is a good document, it is equally allowable, in that situation, to say that the Constitution is a bad document. If a public building may be used in which to say, in time of war, that the war is justified, then the same building may be used in which to say that it is not justified. If it be publicly argued that conscription for armed service is moral and necessary, it may be likewise publicly argued that it is immoral and unnecessary. If it may be said that American political institutions are superior to those of England or Russia or Germany, it may, with equal freedom, be said that those of England or Russia or Germany are superior to ours. These conflicting views may be expressed, must be expressed, not because they are valid, but because they are relevant. If they are responsibly entertained by anyone, we, the voters, need to hear them. When a question of policy is "before the house," free men choose to meet it, not with their eyes shut, but with their eyes open. To be afraid of any idea is to be unfit for self-government. Any such suppression of ideas about the common good, the First Amendment condemns with its absolute disapproval. The freedom of ideas shall not be abridged.

SECTION II

THE FREEDOM OF SCHOLARS AND TEACHERS

A. The Teaching of Intellectual Freedom (1952)

THE PURPOSE of this paper is to state a problem. I have no expectation of reaching a solution of it. I shall be well content if, at the end of the paper, you will recognize my difficulty as falling within the field of your activities and will feel the need of doing something about it.

The problem is suggested by the recent happenings at the University of California. As a retired professor, living in Berkeley beside the university, I have watched with deep concern the disastrous conflict which has raged in that institution during the last two or three years. It is out of a sympathetic sharing in the agonies of that conflict that I am seeking its sources and am presenting for your consideration one of the most perplexing aspects of the work done in our universities and colleges.

Though my own judgment of the rights and wrongs of the California dispute is that of a partisan who condemns the action of the Regents and applauds, especially, the resistance of the nonsigners who refuse to obey the Regents' edict, the question which I have in mind does not concern that specific issue. I am thinking rather of a deeper problem which underlies the California quarrel and all other like quarrels in our institutions of higher learning. It is the question of our responsibility for the teaching of intellectual freedom to the people of the United States. Have we such a responsibility? If so, what is it? Do we meet it, or fail to meet it? I am asking, you see, about the func-

tional relation between the scholars and teachers of the nation
and that combination of economic, political, social, moral, aes-
thetic, and intellectual activities which, taken together, we popu-
larly call the American Way of Life.

1

Thirty-seven years ago, your Association was formed in the
interest of professional development. A necessary condition of
professional development, as the founders of the Association
clearly perceived, was the establishment of some degree of academic self-government. In those far-off days, which most of you
are too young to remember, a group of keen and generous minds,
with many of whom I had personal friendship, had perceived a
danger which increasingly threatened the integrity and effectiveness of the work done in our colleges and universities. They saw
that, by a process of events for which no one could be held responsible, the control and administration of research and teaching
were passing over into the hands of non-academic men. I shall
not try to specify the forces which were driving in that direction.
For my present purpose, it is enough to note that the founders of
your Association saw the drift, and judged it to be dangerous.
And their response to that danger was the suggestion that the
faculties of colleges and universities should be given, and should
exercise, certain kinds of authority for determining the aims of
research and teaching, and for making sure that, in actual procedures, those aims were realized.

The argument of this paper will not discuss the career of your
Association in the pursuit of that immediate intention. As an outsider, I cannot claim competence for that task nor would it be
seemly that, on this occasion, I attempt it. There are, however,
two brief remarks about it which, on the way to my theme, I wish
to make in passing. First, the judgment from which the Association sprang was, I am sure, valid. There was, and is, a drift, a
danger, which makes it imperative that effective control of

academic work shall be in the hands of the women and men who are doing that work. And second, as judged by its own intention, you seem to me to have won unexpected success. You have not beaten down the forces which, more or less blindly, threaten freedom. At no point in our common life has that been done. But in the midst of conflict, you have held your ground without retreat. You have proclaimed what research and teaching are, and why, in their fundamental aspects, they must govern themselves. I am not saying that your words have been fully understood. I do say that you have spoken the truth.

But, as already suggested, the inquiry which I now venture to present to you is not primarily concerned with the freedom and self-government of the professors of the United States. It is concerned, rather, with the freedom and self-government of the people of the United States. You and I know that neither research nor teaching can be properly done unless it is free. But it is equally true that in the provisions of the Constitution of the United States, the self-governing people of the nation are assigned an intellectual task which, again, cannot be properly done unless the doing of it is free. That demand for the inviolability of the freedom of mind of the members of our body-politic is recognized and formulated in the First Amendment to the Constitution, when it says: "Congress shall make no law respecting an establishment of religion, or prohibiting the free exercise thereof; or abridging the freedom of speech, or of the press; or the right of the people peaceably to assemble, and to petition the Government for a redress of grievances."

Now the issue which I seek to present to you will come to light if we note the identity of intention between the recommendations made by your Association during the past thirty-seven years and the provisions of the First Amendment, which was enacted one hundred sixty-one years ago. In both cases it is demanded that the authority of a legally superior governing agency shall be kept within a defined limit. The agency which governs the colleges and universities is the Regents or Trustees, with their executive officers, including the President. In the case of the nation, the corresponding governing agency is the Congress and, by implication, its executive and judicial associates. In both cases, the governing bodies are given legal authority to provide for the security and welfare of the institutions committed to their care. But also, in both cases alike, they are forbidden to use, in the doing of their work, any abridgment of intellectual freedom. There are many practical devices which they may use. But that device, however immediately useful it might be, they may never use.

Here, then, is the question which I ask you to consider. What is the relation between the freedom of mind of the professor, as defined by your Association, and the freedom of mind of the people, as defined by the First Amendment? And the answer which I suggest is that academic freedom is a special form, a sub-form, of popular freedom. We who engage in research and teaching do so as agents of the people of the nation. In virtue of special abilities and training, we are commissioned to carry on for the people forms of intellectual activity which belong to them, are done in their interest, but which, in some specific forms, they cannot carry on for themselves. Just as some men make shoes and other men grow food, so it is our business to discover truth in its more intellectualized forms and to make it powerful in the guidance of the life of the community. And since we are thus acting as the agents of the people, they grant to us such of their freedom as is needed in that field of work. In a word, the final justification of our academic freedom is to be found not in our purposes but in theirs. In the last resort, it is granted not because we want it or enjoy it, but because those by whom we are commissioned need intellectual leadership in the thinking which a free society must do. May I state the principle bluntly and frankly? Our final responsibility, as scholars and teachers, is not to the truth. It is to the people who need the truth.

2

And now, finally, the argument returns to your Association and to the responsibility of our colleges and universities for the teaching of intellectual freedom to the people of the United States. If what I have said about our plan of government is true, there can be no doubt that the citizens of this nation need that teaching. Without it, the program of self-government is doomed to futility and disaster. But in the face of that necessity, it seems equally true that our scholars and teachers are not providing the teaching which is needed. They are doing something else, and doing it well. But they are not giving the intellectual leadership in freedom upon which the success of the great experiment in self-government depends.

It is at this point that the conflict at the University of California seems to me peculiarly illuminating, because of the striking evidence which it gives in support of the accusation just made. Many tragic facts of suffering and of injustice have marked the course of that conflict. But more tragic than any or all of them is the prior fact that, in this experience, the university has been reaping the bitter fruits of its own planting. When the scholars and teachers of the university have now spoken of the freedom needed in the work they have to do, their words have seemed meaningless, and even absurd, to the people for whom that work is done. Californians, on the whole, have felt the force, the threat, of the protest by the professors. But they have not understood its reasoning, its logic. They have been shocked by the resignations of faculty men of high repute, by the refusal of invitations to men in other universities, and by the condemnations of learned societies. But they have seemed wholly unable to comprehend why such actions are taken. The academic protest against the requirement of a belief-oath is, for them, a vagary of the professorial mind, rather than an expression of loyalty to a kind of freedom upon which the integrity of free learning in a free society depends.

May I try to depict that basic failure of the teaching of the university—and then my paper will be done.

As you well know, when the California Regents added to the customary loyalty-oath a belief-oath of political conformity, the University Senate, with virtual unanimity, entered formal and vigorous protest against that action. The great majority of the faculty, it is true, in the months of controversy which followed, submitted to the Regent decision. That was done, for the most part, I believe, on the mistaken ground that a continuation of the struggle would be harmful to the university. It did not indicate a change of mind as to the unwisdom and injustice of the Regent procedure. And further, a small minority, some thirty-nine non-signers, at the risk of every item of status and of livelihood which they and their families possessed, refused to submit. They stood fast in their disobedience, and on that ground were dismissed from their posts.

What were these faculty men saying about academic freedom, the signers with compromise, the non-signers without compromise? They were, I think, expressing the conviction that an institution which limits intellectual freedom is not a university. They knew that a man who assumes the social responsibilities of a scholar, a teacher, a preacher, must first of all establish, in the minds of the people whom he serves, the assurance, the certainty, that his beliefs, his utterances, are, independently, his own. They must be sure that he is a man whom no one, not even themselves, can compel to believe this or to say that, can forbid to believe that or to say this. Anyone who submits, under pressure, to coercive control over his thought or his speech, ceases to be a scholar searching for the truth, ceases to be a teacher leading his pupils toward honest and fearless inquiry and belief. He becomes a hired man, thinking what he is paid to think, saying what he is hired to say.

But that duty of intellectual freedom, recognized and expressed by the members of the faculty, has been, on the whole, incomprehensible to those to whom, presumably, that faculty is giving intellectual leadership. The Regents have not understood it, and hence have been driven to fury by its defiance of their authority. The administrators have been bewildered and shocked by the resistance of friends and colleagues with whom they had thought themselves to be on terms of good will and common purpose. And the same inability to interpret what the professors were saying has afflicted the general body of the alumni, whom, supposedly, the university had educated, the greater part of the student body whom, presumably, it is educating, and most clearly of all, the people of the state, for whom, and by whose support and authority, the work of the university is done. Only one group responded to the appeal with comprehension of it and with passionate acceptance of it. That badly-betrayed group was the teaching assistants and graduate students who had been looking forward to careers of research and teaching, of honesty and freedom. To them there has come the incalculable damage of bitter discouragement and disillusionment.

3

Here, then, is the tragic failure which you and I must face. Our universities and colleges, whatever else they have accomplished, have failed to meet their deepest obligation. In a society striving to be free, they have not taught what freedom is, nor how it can be won, nor how it can be lost. They have not made clear to our communities why their teachers must be free, nor why they themselves must be free. And that failure, may I say again, is not peculiar to California. In varying degrees, it runs through the work of our colleges and universities from one end of the country to the other. We scholars and teachers who have, rightly, demanded intellectual freedom for ourselves have not explained, either to our pupils or to the community at large, the justification of that demand. We have seemed to be talking about a special privilege of our craft rather than about our obligations to that fundamental freedom which must be possessed and exercised, not only by us, but by every member of a society which is seeking to be self-governed.

The tragic results of that failure of our teaching can be seen if we compare the quality of our present popular thinking about issues of common concern with the high intellectual achievement of the men who devised the Constitution, who discussed the *Federalist* Papers, and who wrote the First Amendment. In that achievement, our forefathers, by the sheer energy of their intelligence, created an idea which, in that form, the world had not known before. But we today have no such bold and independent thinking. We have become timid and defensive. Unlike our forefathers, we Americans now regard the basic problems of government as having been solved for us by our ancestors. And our chief concern is to protect that ancestral heritage from attacks, domestic and foreign. What we now demand of men's minds, therefore, is not the independence which creates insight but the conformity which destroys it. As the owners of a great tradition, we seek, not to produce but to enjoy, not to cultivate but to defend, not to explore but to exploit. By force, by compulsion, we now drive each other into giving to freedom the slavish, timid loyalty which does not dare to ask what, with the passing of time, a changing freedom has become.

Who in our society is primarily responsible for that process of disintegration? In so far as blame can be assigned, it must be laid, first of all, at the door of our colleges and universities. Theirs are the opportunities and the obligations of intellectual leadership. It is they who are the physicians of the mind. As they have failed us, we Americans are in desperate need of the teaching of intellectual freedom. What, I come here to ask this Association, can be done about it?

And now may I quote one last word from Immanuel Kant, who seems to me to have had, more than any other Western thinker, an understanding of the function of the free mind in the life of a society. Looking back upon his own career, Kant said:

I am an investigator by inclination. I feel a great thirst for knowledge and an impatient eagerness to advance, also satisfaction at each progressive step forward. There was a time when I thought that all this could constitute the honor of humanity, and I despised the common people who know nothing about it. Rousseau set me straight. This dazzling excellence vanishes. I learn to honor men, and would consider myself much less useful than common laborers if I did not believe that this purpose gives all the others their value —to establish the rights of humanity.

B. *Professors on Probation* (*1949*)

The President and Regents of the University of Washington have dismissed three professors and have placed three others on probation. That statement fails to mention the most significant feature of what has been done. The entire faculty is now on probation. Every scholar, every teacher, is officially notified that if, in his search for the truth, he finds the policies of the American Communist party to be wise, and acts on that belief, he will be dismissed from the university.

In one of the dismissal cases, the evidence is not clear enough to enable an outsider to measure the validity of the decision. But the other five cases force an issue on which everyone who cares for the integrity and freedom of American scholarship and teaching must take his stand. Cool and careful consideration of that issue should be given by all of us, whether or not we agree with the teachers in question, but especially if we do not agree with them.

The general question in dispute is that of the meaning of academic freedom. But that question has three distinct phases. The first of these has to do with the organization of a university. It asks about the rights and duties of the faculty in relation to the rights and duties of the administration. And the principle at issue corresponds closely to that which, in the government of the

United States, is laid down by the First Amendment to the Constitution. Just as that Amendment declares that "Congress shall make no law abridging the freedom of speech," so, generally, our universities and colleges have adopted a principle which forbids the administration to abridge the intellectual freedom of scholars and teachers. And, at this point, the question is whether or not the President and Regents at Washington have violated an agreement made in good faith and of vital importance to the work of the university.

The principle of academic freedom was clearly stated by Sidney Hook in the *New York Times Magazine* of February 27, 1949. After noting that "administration and trustees" are "harried by pressure-groups," Mr. Hook concluded his argument by saying, "In the last analysis, there is no safer repository of the integrity of teaching and scholarship than the dedicated men and women who constitute the faculties of our colleges and universities." On the basis of that conviction, the Association of University Professors has advocated, and most of our universities, including Washington, have adopted, a "tenure system." That system recognizes that legal authority to appoint, promote, and dismiss teachers belongs to the President and Regents. But so far as dismissals are concerned, the purpose of the tenure agreement is to set definite limits to the exercise of that authority.

This limitation of their power, governing boards throughout the nation have gladly recognized and accepted. To the Association of University Professors it has seemed so important that violations of it have been held to justify a "blacklisting" of a transgressor institution—a recommendation by the association that scholars and teachers refuse to serve in a university or college which has thus broken down the defenses of free inquiry and belief.

It is essential at this point to note the fact that the fear expressed by the tenure system is a fear of action by the President and Regents. Since these officers control the status and the salaries of teachers, it is only through them or by them that effective external pressure can be used to limit faculty freedom. To say then, as we must, that the explicit purpose of the tenure system is to protect freedom against the President and Regents, is not to say that these officials are more evil than others. Theirs is the power by which, unless it is checked by a tenure system, evil may be done.

Under the excellent code adopted at the University of Washington, it is agreed that after a trial period in which the university makes sure that a teacher is competent and worthy of confidence, he is given "permanence" of tenure. This means that he is secure from dismissal unless one or more of five carefully specified charges are proved against him. And the crucial feature of this defense of freedom is that the holding of any set of opinions, however unpopular or unconventional, is scrupulously excluded from the list of proper grounds for dismissal. The teacher who has tenure may, therefore, go fearlessly wherever his search for the truth may lead him. And no officer of the university has authority, openly or by indirection, to abridge that freedom.

When, under the Washington code, charges are made against a teacher, it is provided that prosecution and defense shall be heard by a tenure committee of the faculty, which shall judge whether or not the accusations have been established. In the five cases here under discussion, the only charge made was that of present or past membership in the American Communist Party. Specific evidence of acts revealing unfitness or misconduct in university or other activities was deliberately excluded from the prosecution case. And further, since the alleged fact of party membership was frankly admitted by the defense, the only question at issue was the abstract inquiry whether or not such membership is forbidden under the five provisions of the tenure code.

Upon that issue, the faculty committee decided unanimously that in the cases of the ex-members of the Communist party, there were, under the code, no grounds for dismissal. And by a vote of eight to three, the same conclusion was reached concerning the two men who were still members of the party. In the discussions of the committee, the suggestion was made that the code should be so amended that party membership would give ground for dismissal. But that action was not recommended. In its capacity as the interpreter of the code which now protects academic freedom, the committee, in all five cases, declared the charges to be not supported by the evidence presented.

In response to this judgment upon teachers by their intellectual peers, the Regents, on recommendation of the President, dismissed the two party members. And second, going beyond the recommendation of the President, they placed the three ex-members "on probation" for two years. These actions are clearly a violation of the agreement under which faculty members have accepted or continued service in the university. They deserve the condemnation of everyone who respects the integrity of a covenant, of everyone who values faculty freedom and faculty responsibility for the maintaining of freedom.

The second phase of the general question goes deeper than the forms of university organization. It challenges the wisdom of the tenure code as it now stands. It may be that, though the Regents are wrong in procedure, they are right in principle. Here, then, we must ask whether President Allen is justified in saying that a teacher who is "sincere in his belief in communism" cannot "at the same time be a sincere seeker after truth which is the first obligation of the teacher." In a press interview, Mr. Allen is quoted as saying, "I insist that the Communist party exercises thought control over every one of its members. That's what I object to." Such teachers, he tells us, are "incompetent, intellectually dishonest, and derelict in their duty to find and teach the truth." Can those assertions be verified? If so, then the tenure code should be amended. If not, then the action of the university should be immediately and decisively reversed.

No one can deny that a member of the American Communist Party accepts a "discipline." He follows a party "line." As the policies of the party shift, he shifts with them. That statement is in some measure true of all parties, whose members agree to work together by common tactics toward a common end. But the Communist discipline, it must be added, is unusually rigid and severe. Our question is, then, whether submission to that discipline unfits for university work men who, on grounds of scholarship and character, have been judged by their colleagues to be fitted for it.

For the judging of that issue we must examine the forces by means of which the discipline of the American Communist Party is exercised. It is idle to speak of "thought control" except as we measure the compulsions by which that control is made effective. What then are the inducements, the dominations, which by their impact upon the minds of these university teachers, rob them of the scholar's proper objectivity?

So far as inducements are concerned, good measuring of them requires that we place side by side the advantages offered to a scholar by the Communist Party and those offered by the President and Regents of a university. On the one hand, as seen in the present case, the administration can break a man's career at one stroke. It has power over every external thing he cares for. It can destroy his means of livelihood, can thwart his deepest inclinations and intentions. For example, in very many of our universities it is today taken for granted that a young scholar who is known to be a Communist has not the slightest chance of a faculty appointment. He is barred from academic work. And, as against this, what has the American Communist Party to offer? Its "inducements" are the torments of suspicion, disrepute, insecurity, personal and family disaster.

Why then do men and women of scholarly training and taste choose party membership? Undoubtedly, some of them are, hysterically, attracted by disrepute and disaster. But, in general, the only explanation which fits the facts is that these scholars are moved by a passionate determination to follow the truth where it seems to lead, no matter what may be the cost to themselves and their families. If anyone wishes to unearth the "inducements" which threaten the integrity of American scholarship he can find

far more fruitful lines of inquiry than that taken by the administration of the University of Washington.

But Communist controls, we are told, go far deeper than
"inducements." The members of the party, it is said, "take orders
from Moscow"; they are subject to "thought control by a foreign
power." Now here again, the fact of rigid party discipline makes
these assertions, in some ambiguous sense, true. But, in the sense
in which President Allen and his Regents interpret them, they are
radically false.

Let us assume as valid the statement that, in the American
Communist Party "orders" do come from Moscow. But by what
power are those orders enforced in the United States? In the
Soviet Union, Mr. Stalin and his colleagues can, and do, enforce
orders by police and military might. But by what form of "might"
do they control an American teacher in an American university?
What can they do to him? At its extreme limit, their only enforcing action is that of dismissal from the party. They can say to him,
"You cannot be a member of this party unless you believe our
doctrines, unless you conform to our policies." But, under that
form of control, a man's acceptance of doctrines and policies is
not "required." It is voluntary.

To say that beliefs are required as "conditions of membership"
in a party is not to say that the beliefs are required by force,
unless it is shown that membership in the party is enforced. If
membership is free, then the beliefs are free.

Misled by the hatreds and fears of the cold war, President Allen
and his Regents are unconsciously tricked by the ambiguities of
the words "control" and "require" and "free" and "objective."
The scholars whom they condemn are, so far as the evidence
shows, free American citizens. For purposes of social action, they
have chosen party affiliation with other men, here and abroad,
whose beliefs are akin to their own. In a word, they do not accept
Communist beliefs because they are members of the party. They
are members of the party because they accept Communist beliefs.

Specific evidence to support the assertion just made was staring President Allen and his Regents in the face at the very time when they were abstractly denying that such evidence could exist. Three of the five men whom they condemned as enslaved by party orders had already, by their own free and independent thinking, resigned from the party. How could they have done that if, as charged, they were incapable of free and independent thinking? Slaves do not resign.

At the committee hearings, these men explained, simply and directly, that under past conditions, they had found the party the most effective available weapon for attack upon evil social forces, but that with changing conditions, the use of that weapon seemed no longer advisable. Shall we say that the decision to be in the party gave evidence of a lack of objectivity while the decision to resign gave evidence of the possession of it? Such a statement would have no meaning except as indicating our own lack of objectivity.

In these three cases, as in the more famous case of Granville Hicks, who some years ago resigned party membership with a brilliant account of his reasons for doing so, the charge made cannot be sustained. The accusation as it stands means nothing more than that the President and Regents are advocating one set of ideas and are banning another. They are attributing to their victims their own intellectual sins. And the tragedy of their action is that it has immeasurably injured the cause which they seek to serve and, correspondingly, has advanced the cause which they are seeking to hold back.

The third phase of our question has to do with the wisdom, the effectiveness, of the educational policy under which teachers have been dismissed or put on probation. And on this issue, the evidence against the President and Regents is clear and decisive. However good their intention, they have made a fatal blunder in teaching method.

As that statement is made, it is taken for granted that the

primary task of education in our colleges and universities is the teaching of the theory and practice of intellectual freedom, as the first principle of the democratic way of life. Whatever else our students may do or fail to do, they must learn what freedom is. They must learn to believe in it, to love it, and most important of all, to trust it.

What then is this faith in freedom, so far as the conflict of opinions is concerned? With respect to the world-wide controversy now raging between the advocates of the freedom of belief and the advocates of suppression of belief, what is our American doctrine? Simply stated, that doctrine expresses our confidence that whenever, in the field of ideas, the advocates of freedom and the advocates of suppression meet in fair and unabridged discussion, freedom will win. If that were not true, if the intellectual program of democracy could not hold its own in fair debate, then that program itself would require of us its own abandonment. That chance we believers in self-government have determined to take. We have put our faith in democracy.

But the President and Regents have, at this point, taken the opposite course. They have gone over to the enemy. They are not willing to give a fair and equal hearing to those who disagree with us. They are convinced that suppression is more effective as an agency of freedom than is freedom itself.

But this procedure violates the one basic principle on which all teaching rests. It is impossible to teach what one does not believe. It is idle to preach what one does not practice. These men who advocate that we do to the Russians what the Russians, if they had the power, would do to us are declaring that the Russians are right and that we are wrong. They practice suppression because they have more faith in the methods of dictatorship than in those of a free self-governing society.

For many years the writer of these words has watched the disastrous educational effects upon student opinion and attitude when suppression has been used, openly or secretly, in our universities and colleges. The outcome is always the same. Dictator-ship breeds rebellion and dissatisfaction. High-spirited youth will not stand the double-dealing which prates of academic freedom and muzzles its teachers by putting them "on probation."

If we suggest to these young people that they believe in democracy, then they will insist on knowing what can be said against it as well as what can be said for it. If we ask them to get ready to lay down their lives in conflict against an enemy, they want to know not only how strong or how weak are the military forces of that enemy, but also what he has to say for himself as against what we are saying for ourselves.

Many of the students in our colleges and universities are today driven into an irresponsible radicalism. But that drive does not come from the critics of our American political institutions. It comes chiefly from the irresponsible defenders of those institutions —the men who make a mockery of freedom by using in its service the forces of suppression.

Underlying and surrounding the Washington controversy is the same controversy as it runs through our national life. The most tragic mistake of the contemporary American mind is its failure to recognize the inherent strength and stability of free institutions when they are true to themselves. Democracy is not a weak and unstable thing which forever needs propping up by the devices of dictatorship. It is the only form of social life and of government which today has assurance of maintaining itself.

As contrasted with it, all governments of suppression are tempo-rary and insecure. The regimes of Hitler and Mussolini flared into strength, and quickly died away. The power of the Soviet Union cannot endure unless that nation can find its way into the practices of political freedom. And all the other dictatorships are falling, and will fall, day by day. Free self-government alone gives promise of permanence and peace. The only real danger which threatens our democracy is that lack of faith which leads us into the devices and follies of suppression.

C. The Integrity of the Universities (1953)

A recent statement issued by the Association of American Universities discusses congressional investigations of the political beliefs and affiliations of teachers in the universities. That statement seems to me to fall into error by ignoring basic features of our American culture which are relevant to that discussion.

1

As the principles and practices of the free mind have been slowly worked out in our democratic society, it has often happened that individuals and institutions devoted to the pursuit of truth have refused to submit to the imposition of ecclesiastical or political controls over personal beliefs or the communication of those beliefs. The issue raised by that refusal has taken one of its most controversial forms when the authorities of Church or State have required, with varying kinds of inquisition, that an individual should make compulsory disclosure of his opinions or of his association with others in the advocacy of those opinions. Over and over again, in the history of our Western society, individuals and groups have challenged that requirement, have decided, even under the threat of severe penalties, that they could not loyally submit to it.

In the course of the long struggle against suppression, individual freedom has won great victories. Both the churches and the universities have fought for and have secured decisive limitations of the jurisdiction of legislative and other governing agencies. The greatest of all among those victories is recorded in the First Amendment to our Constitution by which our own government forbids its Congress to take any action which would abridge the freedom of religion, speech, press, assembly, or petition. The basic meaning of that enactment is that all citizens, scholars or nonscholars, as they deal with the issues of religion or of politics, shall be unhindered by the intimidation or control of any governing agency. They must be free to follow the truth wherever it may seem to them to lead.

The most striking contribution of the universities to the winning of the freedom of the mind is, however, that they have gone far beyond mere resistance to the external authority of the civil government. They have also, following the lead of the federal government, limited the use of their own authority. They have seen that, in universities as they are now organized, administrative actions upon appointments, salaries, promotions, dismissals, and so on, might be used, consciously or unconsciously, to influence and control the opinions and expressions of scholars and teachers. And since nothing worse than this could happen to a university, they have taken careful precautions against such abuse of their own powers. Those precautionary self-limitations are what we call "the system of academic tenure." Their purpose is not to grant special favors to faculty members. It is to guard the independence and integrity of the university's own work.

The tenure system, as usually adopted, makes two sets of provisions. First, it arranges that no one shall be given "permanent tenure" on the teaching staff until his moral and intellectual competence has been tested and approved by his colleagues, on the basis of years of active service. But second, when permanent status is thus granted to a professor, it is also provided that no adverse action shall be taken against him, except on charges of moral or intellectual incompetence, carefully defined in advance and carefully investigated by competent colleagues. These provisions give assurance that neither the threat of dismissal nor of any other administrative action will ever be used to terrify faculty members, to impose upon them an intellectual or religious or political orthodoxy. An institution which would require such orthodoxy could not be a university—that is what the Tenure System means.

2

The immediate crisis which has called forth the statement of
the Association of American Universities arises from the fact that
committees of the federal legislature are now attempting to impose
upon faculty members the demand that they make compulsory
disclosure of their beliefs and associations. And some of the
scholars and teachers who have been questioned under this procedure have refused to "cooperate," have denied the authority of
the committees to demand an answer to their questions. These
"protestants" have, therefore, been held to be in "contempt" of
Congress and have been recommended for prosecution and, if
convicted, for punishment. Where that situation has arisen, what
is the duty of a university toward a "protesting" professor to
whom it has granted permanent tenure? That is the basic question with which the statement of the universities is called upon to
deal. As a reader seeks to assess the validity of the statement's
answer, the following factors seem relevant and are, I think,
decisive.

It must, of course, be recognized that the refusal to "cooperate"
with a governing agency will incur popular disapproval. The
beliefs under investigation are, generally, regarded as dangerous
and evil. A protestant's refusal to share in what seems to him a
futile or unconstitutional method of rooting them out arouses,
therefore, a double hostility. It outrages prevailing anxieties. It
appears to defy established authority. For the reason just stated,
it is sometimes suggested that a teacher who holds fast to his conviction that legislative committees are exceeding their authority is
thereby doing harm to his university by arousing resentment
against it. But in reply to that it must be said that no university
can play its proper part in the life of a community unless it can
be trusted to meet such resentments without terror, without
yielding because of terror. And further, it must be said that the
only serious injury which any teacher can do to his university is

that he submit his mind or his words to external domination, whether by the government or any other institution—that he think what he is required to think, that he say what he is required to say.

But the decisive element in the situation is the claim that a citizen-scholar of the United States may honestly, intelligently, loyally believe that the intent of the Constitution forbids him to submit to the requirement of compulsory disclosure of his beliefs. The question of the constitutional relation between a citizen and his legislature is as difficult as it is important. Men technically trained in law, or not so trained, may and do differ about it honestly, intelligently, loyally. And, that being true, it can never be validly said that adherence to either side of the issue gives evidence, by itself, of moral or intellectual incompetence.

From what has just been said it follows that no university is called upon to decide whether a protesting professor is right or wrong in his refusal to "cooperate." Any genuine institution of learning accepts diversity of opinion on such controversial issues as a fruitful feature of its work. And this means that, for an institution which has adopted a tenure system, the only relevant question is "Has this man, by his protest, given evidence of any of those forms of moral or intellectual incompetence which are agreed upon as the only justifications of disciplinary action against him?" If such evidence is lacking, a genuine university will stand by its accredited representative, as it is pledged to do. And if any other agency, governmental or non-governmental, attempts to discipline him, such a university will not supinely acquiesce, will not consent to or share in the violation of those principles upon which its very existence, as a servant of the truth, depends.

3

As against the attitude thus far defined, the statement of the universities seems to me to deny and discard the meaning of the

Constitution about intellectual freedom, to deny and discard, also, the application of that meaning which is formulated by the tenure system. That position, taken by the statement in reference to the protesting professor, reads as follows: "It is his duty as a citizen and a professor to speak out if he is called upon to answer for his convictions. Refusal to do so, on whatever legal grounds, cannot fail to reflect upon a profession that claims for itself the fullest freedom to speak, and the maximum protection of that freedom available in our society."

Is it true that an American citizen-scholar may be "called upon to answer for his convictions"? Does a teacher who honestly, intelligently, loyally, stands fast, under pressure, by his conviction as to the meaning of the Constitution and the obligations of a scholar, thereby "reflect upon" his "profession"?

As against such pronouncements as these the universities, rising to the defense of the men whom they have found worthy of trust, should be saying to committees which have transformed investigation into inquisition, "We have tested these men in adequate ways, and we know them to be morally and intellectually fitted for our work. Nothing which you have alleged about them gives reason for the withdrawing of that judgment. If, then, you bring legal action against them, we will take part in their legal defense. If you succeed in convicting them, we will do everything in our power to secure reversal of that conviction by higher courts. If they are sent to jail, we will keep them on our rolls and will pay their salaries. And further, when they have taken their punishment, they will find their positions waiting for them among colleagues who, being competent to make such a judgment, will gladly recognize them as fellow-workers in the research and teaching of a free society."

I wish the universities were saying something like that rather than what they have said. The nation desperately needs their leadership in the cultivation and defense of individual freedom.

The battle for that freedom cannot be won merely by the martyrdom of individual scholars. Each university must stand fast as a unit, and all the universities must stand together in defense of the principle which makes a university what it is, which defines its deepest obligation to the nation which it serves.

LEGISLATIVE INVESTIGATION OF POLITICAL

BELIEFS AND ASSOCIATIONS

A. Letter to the Harvard Crimson *in reply to a letter from Professors Chafee and Sutherland (1953)*

To the Editor of the *Harvard Crimson*

Dear Sir:

On January 13, 1953, you published a letter from Professors Chafee and Sutherland of the Harvard Law School. Its purpose was to consider "the use and the limitations of the privilege against self-incrimination contained in the Fifth Amendment— 'No person . . . shall be compelled in any criminal case to be a witness against himself. . . .' "

The obverse side of that issue is, just now, that of "the use and the limitations" of the authority of Congressional committees. And in the discussions of that theme, the *Crimson* letter seems to me to have had more influence than any other public statement. Unfortunately, that influence has been, I think, misleading. The writers of your letter are deservedly held in such high esteem that this opinion of mine must, I fear, appear ill-founded. I would like, however, to try to say what can be said in its behalf.

1

The argument of the letter begins as follows: "The underlying principle to remember in considering the subject is the duty of the citizen to cooperate in government. He has no option to say, 'I do not approve of this Grand Jury or that Congressional Committee; I dislike its members and its objectives; therefore, I will not tell what I know.' "

That statement of the underlying issue is, I think, confusing. The assertion that it is the duty of a citizen to "cooperate in government" is, in some sense, true. But in what sense? Is a refusal, on Constitutional grounds, to give information to a committee of Congress, as such, a refusal of "cooperation in government"? If so, what shall we say of the "checks and balances" which are said to characterize our political institutions? The President of the United States has, on occasion, clashed with Congressional committees on this issue, has denied their demand for information from his files. So too, in recent controversies, have the Departments of State, Justice, and War. Have they, then, failed in their "duty to cooperate in government"? Or have they rather expressed their loyalty to our plan of government by refusing to submit to the demands of a legislature which in their opinion is usurping powers which are specifically denied to it by the Constitution?

The plain fact is that, in the give and take of our political life, the duty of refusing to submit to Congressional demands is quite as firmly, though not so widely, established as is the duty of submitting to those demands. And that duty is laid upon the citizens of a free society as directly and inescapably as upon their representatives. Men cannot have political self-government unless they too, as citizens, take on political responsibilities. And, as Alexander Hamilton tells in the *Federalist,* one of their most urgent duties as they "cooperate in government" is to keep an ever-threatening legislature within the limits which the citizens themselves have established in their Constitution.

2

Having thus defined its "underlying" principle, the letter next proceeds to say:

"To this general duty of the citizen the privilege against self-incrimination is an extraordinary exception."

As we read that "general" statement, we should remember that the First Amendment also places limitations upon legislative authority, which are even more "extraordinary" than are those of the Fifth. And this means that the duty of submission to Congress is not so "general" as the letter suggests. In fact, Constitutional restrictions upon Congressional power are not exceptional. And especially when the freedom of political opinion or affiliation is at stake, those restrictions express the essential purpose, the most "general" meaning, of our plan of government. In that plan, the control of the citizens over Congress is far more fundamental than is the control of Congress over the citizens.

3

As it considers the crucial question: "Who shall decide whether or not it is the duty of a citizen to answer questions asked by a Congressional committee?" the *Crimson* letter accepts the well-established thesis that the Fifth Amendment applies to such questioning as well as to the various forms of judicial proceedings for the investigation of crime.

Two conclusions are offered as the outcome of the discussion. First, it is argued that the final authority to decide whether or not a citizen shall answer questions asked by a committee belongs, not to the citizen, but to the committee. Second, on that assumption, citizens are advised to answer questions "frankly and honestly."

May I, in advance, venture the opinion that the arguing is not valid and that the advice is contrary to sound public policy?

4

The contention of the argument is stated as follows:

The witness is not the ultimate judge of the tendency of an answer to incriminate him. He can be required, on pain of contempt punishment, to disclose enough to show a real possibility that an answer to the question will tend, rightly or wrongly, to convict him of a crime. Manifestly this is a delicate business. The witness must not be required to prove his guilt in demonstrating the incriminating character of the answer sought. A judge must decide when the witness nas gone far enough to demonstrate his peril.

The first sentence of that statement tells us that in a criminal proceeding the judge, rather than the witness himself, has authority to decide whether or not a "witness" shall testify. And from this it is argued that the "witness" in a Congressional investigation is, in the same way, subject to the decision of the committee, rather than to his own, on the issue as to whether or not he shall answer questions. But the flaw in that argument is that the word "witness" has changed meaning as the inference passes from premise to conclusion. In the premise the witness is a person who gives evidence about someone else, *viz.* the defendant. In the conclusion, the witness is, in the crucial cases, a person who is asked to give evidence about himself. He is the defendant. And the privilege of "testimonial silence" which the Fifth Amendment provides takes two very different forms when accorded to those two very different persons. It is that very significant difference of which the *Crimson* letter fails to take account.

What, then, is the difference? When, in a legal proceeding, a person is held on suspicion or is tried by a court, other persons may legally be called as "witnesses" and compelled to give evidence for or against him. And these "witnesses" are, with respect to the giving of testimony, subject to that authority of the judge of which the letter speaks. But is it likewise true, in a court of justice, that the judge is empowered to decide whether or not the "defendant" shall give testimony? Presumably the defendant is capable of being a witness. He has, or may have, information which prosecution and judge and jury could use. May he, then, be required to take the witness stand and give that information? Certainly not! In a criminal proceeding at any level, the defendant himself, with such advice as he may take from his lawyer, is "the ultimate judge" as to whether or not he shall testify. Neither the prosecution nor the judge has authority in the matter. And further, he does not, at this point, enter a plea. He makes a decision, and to interpret that decision, if it is against testifying, as a plea for freedom from self-incrimination is to so falsify the defendant's privilege of silence as to destroy both its meaning and its effectiveness. The argument presented by Professors Chafee and Sutherland fails because it ignores the fact that, historically and logically, the Fifth Amendment has two purposes, rather than only one. Its primary purpose is to protect a "defendant." Its secondary and derivative purpose is to defend a "witness." To the latter it gives assurance that he need not give any evidence which will incriminate him. To the former it says, "You need not give any evidence at all."

5

Now the letter under discussion speaks of the persons who are subpoenaed by Congressional Committees as "witnesses." Are they, for the most part, witnesses? Or are they defendants? A partial answer to that question is given by an Associated Press dispatch of September 18, which reads as follows:

> Edward Rothschild, Government Printing Office bookbinder, refused to say whether he was a Communist, stole a secret code, or engaged in espionage. He was suspended from his job within an hour.
>
> Rothschild was summoned before the Senate Investigations Subcommittee to face what Chairman Joseph McCarthy (Rep.—Wis.)

said were "some of the most serious charges ever made against a Government official."

McCarthy was sitting as a one-man committee.

"Mr. Rothschild," the Senator said, "very, very serious charges have been made concerning you. That you have been a long-time member of the Communist Party, that you have stolen secret documents, that your wife has been a member and officer of the Communist Party."

He offered the slender pipe-smoking witness a chance to comment at any length. Rothschild shook his head in refusal.

Confronted with a long list of specific questions about Communism and stealing secret papers sent to the Government's big printing plant for printing, Rothschild invoked the Constitution's Fifth Amendment. He said replies might tend to incriminate him.

Turning to Roy Cohn, the subcommittee counsel sitting by his side, Mr. McCarthy issued these instructions:

"Mr. Counsel, will you call the head of the Government Printing Office and tell him of this testimony? I assume he will be suspended. I can't conceive of his being allowed to go back to the Government Printing Office and allowed to handle secret material."

David Schine, a subcommittee staff member, hustled to a telephone booth in the corner of the big hearing room in the Senate Office Building. It wasn't long before McCarthy told reporters word had come back from Philip L. Cole, deputy public printer, that Rothschild had been suspended immediately without pay.

As that all too familiar story goes, Mr. Rothschild was legally justified when he "shook his head in refusal." Under the actual circumstances, his appeal to the Fifth Amendment was also valid. But he was mistaken, or badly advised, when he translated that appeal into a demand for "freedom from self-incrimination." Senator McCarthy was making charges against him, threatening punishment, pronouncing sentence, and getting it executed. He was compelling, not the evidence of a witness, but the confession of a culprit. In the face of that unlawful demand, the Constitution gives to the defendant a privilege. What it authorizes him to

say is not, "I will not incriminate myself" but rather, "You have
no right to ask the question."

But the Fifth Amendment, when combined with other provisions of the Constitution, and especially with the First Amendment, does more than confer a privilege. It also requires of a
defendant the performance of a duty. It is the duty of "active
cooperation in government" which is laid upon every loyal citizen
of the United States. It is the obligation of maintaining freedom
for all citizens by refusing to submit to those legislative usurpations of power by which our American liberties—in violation of
the Constitution which we are pledged to defend—are now being
threatened and destroyed.

6

The "advice" given by the letter is stated as follows:

It is not only a legal requirement but also a principle of wisdom
and good citizenship for an individual called before a court, grand
jury, or a legislative investigating committee to answer questions
frankly and honestly. The constitutional privilege to keep silent is an
exception to the legal obligation to testify; but even when the legal
privilege is available, there are times when it is best not exercised.

The suggestion that every suspect or defendant in a criminal
proceeding is "legally required" to "answer questions frankly and
honestly" is, to say the least, a startling one. But the wide and
debatable generalization here advanced goes far beyond the limits
of the present inquiry. Our field of interest is determined by the
fact that Congressional committees are seeking to compel American citizens to give testimony about their political beliefs and
affiliations. And in that field, the Fifth and the First Amendments
are joined together, as their motives have been joined for centuries, in requiring of free citizens and of free institutions that they
resist with all their might the irresponsible usurpations of a
legislature which would attempt to tell men what they may believe

and what they may not believe, with whom they may associate and with whom they may not associate.

And further, the "advice" of the letter seems to me ill-advised chiefly because it thinks of the defendant merely as a servant of the laws of the legislature, ignoring the fact that he is also a master of them. It talks about him as if he were merely seeking for a "privilege" which will get him out of trouble, but it ignores the free citizenship which requires of him a sense of duty and loyalty to stand fast at whatever cost, in defense of the Constitution to which he has pledged his allegiance.

The final issue here touched upon could be, and should be, argued at great length by all Americans. For the present, however, it is sufficient to call attention to the relation between the *Crimson* letter and the statement on "The Rights and Responsibilities of Universities and Their Faculties," issued by the Association of American Universities on March 30. I would not, for a moment, question the good intentions of the forty-three administrators who approved that statement. And yet their repudiation of the obligations of their intellectual leadership in the nation is one of the most destructive actions in the history of American education. And that repudiation takes its cue directly from the argument and the advice which Professors Chafee and Sutherland have given. The meaning of their letter can be seen most clearly in the sanction which it gives to the action of the Presidents. And the meaning of that action, in turn, can be seen most clearly in the rising fury of suppression which, both in governmental procedures and in private attitudes, is destroying our freedom.

October 10, 1953   ALEXANDER MEIKLEJOHN

*B. Petition for redress of grievance, addressed to the Speaker of
the House of Representatives (1957)*

To the Speaker of the House of Representatives

Dear Mr. Rayburn:

As a citizen of the United States, I hereby respectfully ask that
you present to the House of Representatives this petition for
redress of grievance.

The grievance arises from a House Resolution of 1938, which
created and authorized a Committee on Un-American Activities.
This petition is concerned only with that feature of the Committee's work which the Watkins opinion of the Supreme Court
describes as "the summoning of a witness and compelling him to
testify, against his will, about his beliefs, expressions or associations." Under the Constitution neither the House nor its Committee has authority to "compel testimony" in an area within
which the First Amendment explicitly forbids Congressional
abridgment of political freedom.

It is not the intent of this petition to question the authority of
the House to collect, and to interpret for legislative purposes, information concerning the "beliefs, expressions or associations" of free
men. But the First Amendment sharply limits the scope within
which that authority may be exercised. It forbids Congress, in its
search for needed information, to use compulsions which abridge
the freedom of speech, press, assembly, or petition. I am asking
therefore, that the House, in granting authority to its committees,
shall conform to this limitation which the First Amendment
imposes upon Congressional action. In support of that petition, I
offer, for consideration by the House, the following matters of
fact and of opinion.

First, it is very significant that in the Watkins case, the Supreme
Court has reversed the conviction of a citizen whom, on the

ground that he had refused to submit to the compulsion of the Committee, the House had cited for contempt. But even more significant is the fact that, in reaching this decision, the opinion of the Court, speaking on Constitutional grounds, expressed disapproval both of the specific procedures of the Committee and of the Resolution of 1938 under which the Committee was first created and its authority defined.

Second, the attempt to "compel testimony" in the area of the First Amendment has proved to be, in actual practice, not only unconstitutional, but also ineffectual or harmful. Many of the "witnesses," when called upon to waive their immunities as American citizens, have refused to do so. They have become "unfriendly" witnesses, denying the authority of the Committee to use such compulsion. In these cases, the Committee has known, in advance of its inquiry, that the information asked for would not be given. And for this reason, the only significant outcome of the Committee's use of coercion has been that of "exposing" to public calumny and private disaster citizens of the United States against whom no charges of unlawful action have been proved, or even legally made. Concerning that procedure the Watkins opinion, after a careful discussion of the limits of legislative "compulsory process," says—

"We have no doubt that there is no Congressional power to expose for the sake of exposure. The public is, of course, entitled to be informed concerning the workings of its Government. That cannot be inflated into a general power to expose where the predominant result can only be an invasion of the private rights of individuals."

Mr. Speaker and Members of the House, the considerations here suggested make it clear that the Mandate of the Committee on Un-American Activities, and the procedures under it, have brought into confusion, and even into disrepute, the activities of Congressional investigation upon which the making of our laws largely depends. And this mistake is not a new one in our national history. In several earlier periods, when stirred by the anxieties of war, or the after-effects of war, we have engaged in acts of unconstitutional repression which, when sober judgment returned, we have bitterly repented. The time has come when, once more, by decisive action, we must give clear assurance to ourselves, as well as to the people of other nations, that we have not lost faith in the effectiveness and the wisdom of the principles upon which our Constitution is established.

I, therefore, petition the House of Representatives either (1) to decide against continuing the Mandate of the Committee on Un-American Activities or (2) to so modify that Mandate as to deny to the Committee any authority to "compel testimony" concerning the "beliefs, expressions or associations" of its witnesses.

Hoping that the House will listen to the grievance here stated and will proceed to redress it, I am

Respectfully yours,

December 12, 1957   ALEXANDER MEIKLEJOHN

POSTSCRIPT

THIS BOOK has attempted to interpret the intention and the general provisions of the Constitution, so far as they relate to that self-government which is our political freedom. And now, with basic abstractions tentatively defined, common sense requires that a citizen of the United States should face and grapple with the more concrete issues suggested by Professor Sharp in his Foreword. Under the actual conditions of life in the United States does the Constitution work well? Does it provide wise and efficient guidance for our dealing with the desperate issues which are now, in ever-new forms, rushing upon the nation? If not, should it be amended or even abandoned? What alternative lines of Constitutional planning, if any, give promise of providing better care for the national welfare? Or, as against all these suggestions, may we decide that the source of our political difficulties lies not in the Constitution, but in ourselves? Have we unwittingly fallen into a way of life which is inherently hostile both to the Constitution and to the human values which it seeks to enhance and preserve? If so, how shall we change that way of life to make it promote, rather than prevent, the creation of freedom?

As my good friend, former pupil, and present teacher intimates, the inquiry of two decades, as reported in these pages, has not dealt directly with any of these "practical" problems. It has tried to do nothing more than to clear the ground for the struggle to solve them. And the writer of this book is pragmatic enough to believe that abstract reasoning which does not contribute to the removing of the difficulties and the realizing of the purposes out

159

of which it arises, is worthless. And yet it must be said with equal emphasis that no form of action is more inefficient and self-defeating than that which—refusing to abstract principles from their concrete settings—undertakes to manage practical affairs one by one, without searching out the general ideas of fact and value which, interpreting those affairs, give them meaning for one another.

This Postscript, as it takes its stand on that platform, makes no claim that we have answered the questions which Mr. Sharp has suggested. Many decades and much intellectual cooperation will be needed for the carrying on of that enterprise. But out of the argument of the book there seem to run three lines of inquiry along which the search for practical wisdom might proceed.

First, the electoral machinery which, by custom and legislative action, we have imposed upon the Constitution, has been peculiarly unsuccessful in winning our confidence that it is suited to its purpose. The party system, as we use or abuse it, with its conventions and platforms, its campaigning appeals so commonly directed to the self-seeking interests of individuals and groups, does not give the impression that we are a nation of free, self-governing minds thinking loyally and objectively about the common good. On the contrary, it makes of us rather that scrambling collection of "factions" which Jefferson feared and condemned. The term "politics" which, if we are free men, should connote our highest aspirations, our most serious and carefully cultivated thinking, has become a term of reproach and contempt. It speaks of trickery rather than of intelligence. Here is a set of problems which our political scientists should be studying, not merely to find out what our practices are, but rather what they must be if the intention of the Constitution is to be realized. What are the best procedures, we ask them, by which free people may, acting together, govern themselves?

The second question which needs fearless and thorough study concerns education. Can one hundred seventy million people of different racial stocks, of conflicting and changing private interests, of imperfect and impeded communication with one another, learn to think together about the general welfare in such a way that each of them may have a valid sense of responsible sharing in the common enterprise of making and managing a free society? To develop that capacity of mind and will is the primary task of our schools and colleges and, perhaps more important, of our classes in adult education. We Americans lack freedom chiefly because we do not know what it is. And that failure of understanding is not due to a lack of capacity. It is due primarily to a lack of interest in such a reflective or theoretical problem. We are concerned with "making good" with forms of competitive success which, as contrasted with the interpreting and practicing of freedom, are trivial and illusory. Nothing short of a fundamental transformation of the spirit and method of our national education, whether in schools or outside of them, can fit us for the responsibilities of thinking and deciding which the Constitution lays upon us. Here are problems for our teachers in relation to which we seem to fall back more than we go forward.

A third difficulty, which follows closely upon the educational one, is that in the course of our enormous and rapid growth in wealth and power, there has grown up in and around us an "American way of life" which is incongruous with and hostile to the intention of the Constitution. "Free enterprise," so-called, and "self-government" are fundamentally at odds with one another. The nature and source of that incongruity can be seen if we examine closely the double meaning of the word "power" as it is used in discussions of the relations between "the people" and their "government."

The word "power" is used by the Constitution in a very special sense which is foreign to our ordinary non-Constitutional use of the term. When the great document provides that we shall reserve and exercise "power" to govern ourselves, it is speaking only of a political "authority" assigned to us under an agreement as to a "plan of government." But that provision gives no assurance that in the actual course of events, we, the people, are able to do what we are authorized to do. "Power," in the sense of "political authority" is radically different from the "power" of private individuals or groups who have the physical, intellectual, and social strength which are needed to take control over human beings and human situations, and to use them for defined plans and purposes. And in the same way, the possession of power in the second sense gives no assurance that those who exercise it have, or should have, authority to do so.

Now it is very easy for the "realistic" or "pluralistic" scholars, who study American political and social life, to show that at the present time, the mass of the voters, who have political authority, are relatively powerless in the deciding of issues of public policy. The power which controls the nation, those scholars tell us, is held by a vast array of non-official groups and individuals who, through shrewdness and influence in their aggressive self-seeking, use the machinery of the laws and the Constitution, as they use other devices, for the furthering of their own private interests. This is, we are told, the "American way of life." In accordance with it private individuals and groups have at their disposal wealth or knowledge or both of them. And so deeply are their activities entrenched in our customs of action and belief that their energy and enterprise and skill seem to us the most characteristic expressions of the spirit of the nation. These "powers" see what they want, and they are clever in getting it. They fight among themselves continuous battles, in which the casualties are heavy. They also combine together for common action. And it is here— so the pluralistic realists tell us—in the conflicts and alliances of non-political groups and individuals, that public policies are worked out, that the controlling of the nation is done.

Is that the way of life of a self-governing society? No one can doubt that there is much of truth in the portrayal which it gives of the external powers or forces which control our national life. But what does it tell us about our freedom? The story, as it is commonly told, does not mean that the private and self-seeking forces of which it speaks have power to "govern" us. It means only that they can, and do, "control" us. But, so far as that is true, "government," in the sense intended by the Constitution, has ceased to exist. To that extent, the people of the United States are not "governed," either by themselves or by anyone else. And the belief that they are "free" is, in so far, merely a myth by means of which they may be manipulated, cajoled, or driven into acting without knowing what they are doing.

Here then, in the relation between authority and power, is the third inquiry for which this book has tried to clear the ground. We Americans have Constitutional authority to govern ourselves. But we can do so only in so far as our deliberate and informed judgment-making is equipped with the power which is needed to control and direct the pursuit of private interest in whatever way the public welfare may require.

By what practical steps can we make our way toward that far-off goal of political freedom? This book has deliberately held back from consideration of that question. In its closing words, however, it may offer for consideration five opinions, bearing upon the issue, which seem to the writer to be implied by the meaning of the Constitution. They are:

(1) The commonly urged identification of Constitutional freedom with the freedom of business enterprise is an illusion which could be entertained only in a society which is too busy in seeking success to give time or energy to finding out what success is.

(2) As judged by our response to the opportunities and obligations of political freedom, we Americans are not, in effect, a competent body-politic. On the contrary, we are, in many of our moods, an unintelligent and ungovernable mob.

(3) It is not true that the best government is the one which governs least. There is much more truth in the maxim that "Eternal Vigilance is the price of Freedom (Liberty)." No nation can be free unless it is strong enough and active enough to control, whenever necessary, every private individual or group whose action affects the general welfare.

(4) We do not understand what a free government is when

we interpret its making and administering of laws as merely repressive, as merely limiting the actions of men. All the repressive and regulatory activities of the Constitution are incidental and secondary features of a creative, constructive undertaking, namely, that of which its Preamble speaks.

(5) Our greatest present disloyalty to the Constitution lies in the fact that we do not study and criticize it as did the men who devised and adopted it. They met novel and desperate situations by establishing unheard-of and revolutionary forms of government. We too are facing novel and desperate situations. Shall we do as they did, or shall we hate and fear those who follow their example? In the practical answering of that question it will be revealed whether the American experiment in freedom is still going on or has already been abandoned.